HAVE MORE
MONEY NOW

World Wrestling
Entertainment™

HAVE MORE
MONEY NOW

A COMMONSENSE APPROACH TO
FINANCIAL MANAGEMENT

JOHN "BRADSHAW" LAYFIELD

New York   London   Toronto   Sydney   Singapore

World Wrestling
Entertainment™

POCKET BOOKS, a division of Simon & Schuster, Inc.

1230 Avenue of the Americas, New York, NY 10020

This book is a publication of Pocket Books, a division of
Simon & Schuster, Inc., under exclusive license from
World Wrestling Entertainment, Inc.

ISBN: 978-0-7434-6633-2

All photos courtesy John "Bradshaw" Layfield
Book design by Dave Stevenson

First Pocket Books trade paperback printing July 2003

1   3   5   7   9   10   8   6   4   2

POCKET and colophon are registered trademarks of
Simon & Schuster, Inc.

Visit us on the World Wide Web
http://simonsays.com
http://www.wwe.com

Manufactured in the United States of America

For information regarding special discounts for bulk
purchases, please contact Simon & Schuster Special Sales
at 1-800-456-6798 or business@simonandschuster.com

I would like to dedicate this book to my parents.

My dad, Lavelle Layfield, was my hero growing up.
My mom, Mary Layfield, is just simply the greatest woman
I have ever met.
I could never have had a better upbringing or
two better parents. Thank you. I love you.

A separate thank you and acknowledgment
goes to Cody Monk of the Dallas Morning News,
an author in his own right,
who helped me find the words.

CONTENTS

PROLOGUE

BEING POOR AIN'T FUN... STAYING THAT WAY IS STUPID

Life Is about Living

I always have believed that life is about living, not just merely existing.

I don't believe in the austerity preached in some financial books, that you have to save all your money now so that you can have some in retirement. There has to be a middle ground. I don't believe that you should have *nothing* now so that you can have *a lot* later. I don't believe that you have to be *miserable* now so that you can be *happy* later.

I have learned a successful model through life experience—not through a book or attending a lecture or just reading a road map, but by going down the road itself. I smell like smoke because I have been through the fire. I promise I can help you through my life story—the mistakes I made, and the successes I have been fortunate enough to have.

I want to help you. I would love to help everyone to become financially successful; however, some people can't be helped. Not because their situation is hopeless—nothing is hopeless—but because they are just too pigheaded to take advice from anyone. If you are one of these people, thanks for buying my book, but when you end up in debt and in trouble, please don't let the people who seize your assets see my book in your house.

If you are not one of these people, then read on. This book is for you. I hope you enjoy it.

I was very fortunate in my early adulthood to receive a second chance financially. I didn't know I needed a second chance until one lonely Sunday afternoon as I was driving through the state I love so much, my beautiful home state of Texas.

My 1980 Chevy step-side pickup.

Twenty-seven Dollars and a Road Map

It's a good thing I had stopped by the gas station a couple of days earlier. The old blue 1980 Chevrolet step-side pickup truck was full, and I had my fingers crossed that I only needed one tank and one fill-up to drive the 330 miles from San Antonio to Athens, Texas, my home.

It wasn't that I minded stopping to fill up. I love Texas, and especially Texas small towns. I grew up in a small town and still live in one that isn't exactly on the beaten path. My concern was that if I had to stop more than once, I couldn't afford to fill the truck up.

It was the spring of 1992. I had just been fired from my second job in the three years since I left college. I had $27 in my bank account. You read that right. I had barely enough to buy this book. Actually, if this book had been out, maybe I wouldn't have been in the situation I was currently in. As it was, I was cruising—okay, flying—up I-35 with just my thoughts, my truck, an incredibly loud stereo system, and that $27.

Somewhere in the drive, I harkened back to an old Benjamin Franklin quote: "Necessity is the mother of invention." This flashback probably happened somewhere between Georgetown and Killeen.

That Benjamin Franklin quote kept sticking with me. It had grabbed me, and my mind wouldn't let it go. Isn't it amazing how much better you listen when you are in need? I was definitely in need, and this necessity was about to spark a personal change. I realized that I had been playing professional football now for three years and, financially speaking, I had wasted those three years. I was no better off financially than I was when I had left college. I realized at this point what a waste of money that had been. The only good thing was that I had not gotten into debt. However, I had spent everything I had made. I had had a great time. Blowing money usually is fun. I had been to Hawaii, the Grand Caymans, Las Vegas—and I had a huge stereo in my truck, all paid for. The problem was that I only had $27 left over. I had a chance to make the rest of my life better, and I hadn't done it. I priced perfection into my future—that is, everything would always be the same—but it turned out it wasn't to be.

I should have known that football couldn't last forever and that the money would have to end eventually. However, like a lot of young athletes I thought it wouldn't. That day, I realized the importance of saving for the future. Three years before, I had never thought this day would come. Now I had to decide if three years from this day I would again be unprepared, or if I would learn from my mistake and not waste the next three years.

Standing at the Crossroads

It was a very important day for me, a twenty-three-year-old standing flat-footed at the crossroads in my life. I had to make a choice of playing the cards I'd been dealt in the best way possible or feeling sorry for myself and continuing down the same road that had gotten me broke. I decided that being poor ain't fun, and staying that way is stupid.

I didn't consider myself stupid, so I decided that I couldn't remain poor.

The set of cards that life had dealt me that day were not cards that I wanted, but the only option I had was to play the hand dealt to me in the best possible way. Whether these cards are good or bad really doesn't matter; you have to figure out the best way to play them. Griping about the cards, or even the dealer, wasn't going to help me any.

Playing pro football for the San Antonio Riders.

At Least I Was Drafted . . . Barely

That day in the spring of 1992 started like any other had the better part of the last three years. I woke up, knees aching, hung over, and headed to football practice. It was my job. I played professional football for a living, and I was living one of my lifelong goals. I was an offensive tackle for the San Antonio Riders of the World League of American Football. The league consisted of a lot of former NFL players and college players who, for whatever reason, were not on an NFL roster.

I was content making my living playing for the Riders. I had spent the fall of 1990 with the Los Angeles Raiders, and now here I was in this new league. I wasn't getting rich, but I was living just like I wanted to and playing football. I didn't think things could get much better. I came to the World League with the intention of making it back to the NFL, but I was enjoying playing so much, I didn't really care where I played. I was just happy playing. This was all I ever wanted to do.

My first year in San Antonio was 1991, also the league's first year. I had an absolute ball playing football that year. The World League was created very much the way Vince McMahon created the XFL. The entire salary structure was built upon performance and bonuses. It made the guys play harder, and the fans liked that. There were bonuses for starting and for outstanding position performance. I believe the fans really appreciated this format.

To me, the league was a great opportunity and a way for me to continue playing football and making a living at the same time.

In the inaugural season of the WLAF, the league started with a position draft. They drafted 111 offensive linemen.

I was number 108.

My reputation for bad knees and uncertainty about the level of talent that was playing in NCAA Division II football really hurt me. I was just glad I was handed a uniform.

In football, players are measured by where they are on the depth chart. The depth chart lists each position and the starter and backup at each spot. On the offensive line, there are five positions: two tackles, two guards, and a center. So on the depth chart there are 10 spots for offensive linemen.

I was number 11.

I may have gotten the coaches' attention by being the only player on the third team, but I knew that if I was ever going to play in this league and have any modicum of success, I had to do something on the field. The cards I had weren't good, but I was about to make the best of them.

On the third day of camp I got a chance at right tackle. I never believed I had a real fair shot at staying with the Raiders, and being chosen so late in the WLAF draft really burned me up. I decided I had to make a statement and make it early or else my football career would be over.

My knees were bad by this time, and the quickness that I had used to my advantage through my career was gone, but I still had a terrific desire to play. Actually, I am not sure words could describe the desire I had to continue playing. You could take my speed, but you couldn't take my desire to play, and believe me, football is all about desire. A forty time and bench press never once made a football player. You simply can't measure heart, and I had heart to spare. There were guys there that were playing because they didn't know what else to do. I was playing because I loved the game.

Let's Fight

I was going to get noticed this day if I had to fight the whole team, the coaches, and the equipment manager. So I started with the players.

After one play early in practice, I got tied up with the defensive end I was going against. We exchanged words. Briefly. Mostly we threw fists. It was like being alive again—I was on a football field battling, and I loved it. The fight got broken up, and things settled down briefly.

I decided I wasn't done. I don't think he wanted to quit either. So instead of going back to the huddle, we went after each other again. I was really beginning to enjoy this. Finally, we got broken up again briefly. Very briefly.

Coach Mike Riley called for a water break, but I really wasn't thirsty. Apparently, the defensive end wasn't either. This time we really got into it. When they broke us up for a third time, Coach Riley called off practice. I not only got noticed, but I got the guys, and me, out of an extremely hard practice. Pretty good day.

The next morning, I walked into practice almost expecting a message that I had just been cut. Instead, I was greeted with the pleasure of looking at a depth chart with my name in a starting position.

I never let the spot go.

I guess the coaches figured if they just left me there, then I wouldn't feel compelled to fight everyone. I was kind of glad. It had taken half a day to fight just one guy properly, and there were over forty guys on the roster, not counting coaches and the equipment manager. My plan to fight everyone would have taken quite a while to execute.

I was playing the cards dealt to me. There was nothing I could do about my past knee injuries, all I could do was to play as hard as I could with the body I had left. I had no real choice except to figure out my next move. The option of feeling sorry for myself never much fit me. Being drafted number 108 wasn't acceptable to me, but I realized that there was nothing I could do about that. I could do something once I got to training camp, though.

You have to play the cards dealt in the best way possible. Sometimes they are good, sometimes they are bad. It doesn't matter. You have to play what is put in your hand.

My Own Football Card

During the first World League year, we got word that the league was going to make a football card for one player at each position on each team. One offensive lineman, one running back, one wide receiver, and so on. The Riders chose to feature me.

I can't tell you how excited I was to have my own football card. I thought I had made it. My mom certainly thought I had made it. I was playing professional football and even had my own card to prove it. I was so excited about the set that I couldn't wait for it to come out.

My own card and my rapid ascension through the depth chart had me thinking I was going to play football forever. And there was no reason to think otherwise.

The league did pretty well that first year. We weren't the NFL, and we weren't trying to be. We had our niche. We were popular in Europe, where several of the teams were based, and we drew decent enough in the States to provide fans a football fix during the NFL off-season.

After that first year, the NFL decided it needed a stage to develop players already on NFL rosters. The big league started showing a greater interest in the WLAF and began allocating players to our league. These allocated players were the made players. Coaches were told to play these guys. They were there to be developed because some NFL team saw enough in them to make an investment to send them to a developmental spring league.

With the influx on new talent in the World League, those players that were stuck somewhere in the middle got caught in the mix. Still, I didn't think I had anything to worry about. I had played every snap the previous year. I was the San Antonio Riders' offensive lineman representative in the WLAF football card set. I would be fine. So I thought.

I reported to camp in the spring of 1992 feeling as good as I could feel. I was moved to left tackle, something I took as a compliment, since I was now protecting the quarterback's blind side.

You're Cutting Who?

After the first preseason game, I got a message that Coach Riley wanted to see me. I thought a lot of Coach Riley, who later became the head coach of the San Diego Chargers after helping turn around the Oregon State program. He had always been a good friend, a real players' coach. He's a credit to the coaching profession.

I thought I had played well in that game. I had no idea why Coach Riley wanted to see me. For all I knew, he was going to tell me I needed to be at practice early tomorrow for a photo shoot for the new World League card set. Or perhaps I was to be the new centerfold for *Dairy Cow Weekly.*

This wasn't a pleasant meeting. I didn't realize that it was the day final cuts were made. I hadn't paid much attention to it because I didn't figure there was any need to pay attention to it. It was just another day on the calendar to me.

Coach Riley's office was just another room in the San Antonio hotel that doubled as our residence. I walked into his office/bedroom and was told the news. The San Antonio Riders no longer had a need for a six-foot-seven, 300-pound left tackle with bad knees and several broken bones to his credit. I don't know if they felt they had to cut me because of the injuries, or if it was the new role the NFL had taken in the league. Either way, it didn't matter, I was unemployed.

I have a lot of respect for Coach Riley. I could tell it really hurt him to do this. If it didn't hurt him, he sure made it look like it did. He told me my offensive line coach, Jim Gilstrap, wanted to see me before I left to say good-bye. I turned around and left the office/bedroom.

My football career was over.

I had further options to continue to play, but I knew my days were numbered at best. I had to play the cards dealt me. I didn't really like those cards.

I had no idea why I was cut. It was a shock. I'm sure the NFL had something to do with it. I was damaged goods and doing nothing but holding some young guy's spot. Coach Riley didn't tell me that. He didn't have to.

I went back to my room to tell my roommate, Mike Kiselak, other friends, and my dream of playing football good-bye. They all thought I was pulling a prank on them. When they saw me walk out of that hotel with my life packed in a few bags, they realized it wasn't a prank.

I was a casualty of the Turk (the football term for the Grim Reaper).

Out of Money, Out of a Job—
Not a Good Combination

I had budgeted my money perfectly from my first World League season to the next. I didn't worry much about money. I figured I would keep playing forever and make this kind of money forever. I hadn't planned on getting cut. This is a problem with a lot of young men who go into professional sports. All of their lives they are taken care of, and then when they sign a pro contract they are still taken care of. Often the first time they have to face the world by themselves is when they are released from a team. These young guys normally aren't prepared for this. I wasn't either. This is also the first time these young athletes find themselves alone. I was definitely alone.

The positive was that I had accomplished my dream of playing professional football. The negative was, I was driving up I-35 with nothing but my blue pickup, a bunch of construction, and $27 to keep me company. I made just enough to live like I wanted. I didn't live past my means, but I spent everything I made. I priced perfection into my future, believing that my future was going to be as perfect as my present.

It's humbling to realize that you can't afford to live like you have been or buy things that you are used to having. This is called maturing, growing up—we all have to do it. But it sure did stink when I had to do it. Living like a king and not having to grow up, being immature with a pocket full of money, sure was a lot more fun.

Everybody goes through this process at some point. Mine just came much earlier than I wanted or thought it would. Going through this humbles you, but it also makes you take a hard look at reality. I learned this at an early age, and it ended up being the most valuable lesson I ever learned. Had I made it in the NFL, I likely would have ended my career in the same place I was that day I got cut from the Riders. I would be broken down, broke, and left with no second chance at breathing new life into a new career or my finances. I could handle the bad knees. The lack of paycheck was quite depressing.

When I was making that drive up I-35, I didn't know if I'd ever make decent money again. I told myself that three years from that point I was going to be better off than I was currently, even if it was just by a little. Of course, that wouldn't take a whole lot (just $28 in my pocket would be an improvement), but at that time I didn't feel like setting goals too lofty. I know all good things don't have to come to an end, but mine had. I promised myself that if I ever had a chance to make money again, I would not make the same mistake.

My Three Lifelong Goals

I had to have a plan, and a good one. I had set three goals for myself growing up: play football at Abilene Christian University, play professional football, and become rich.

I had come up a little short on the third one.

I have always been competitive and have always tried to work a little smarter, a little longer than the next guy. My current situation was begging for me to take it head on. I was hurt, no question. It was one of the lower points of my life.

The fire, though, still remained. That fire was instilled in me during my early years and on into high school when I began playing football in the ultracompetitive Texas high school ranks.

I was at a huge crossroads in my life. My whole life had been spent playing football and living to play football. It was now coming to an end. Did I try to hang on, or should I do what was best for my future?

My future was bleak in football, but it wasn't elsewhere. I had grown up a wrestling fan. I had always dreamed of being a wrestler. I had just figured I would play football too long to realize that dream. However, now I had the opportunity to do just that. It was still hard to give up on that small-town dream of playing football forever.

High School Football in West Texas

I was raised in Sweetwater, Texas. Sweetwater is just over two hundred miles west from Dallas–Fort Worth. Interstate 20 runs right through the town. With a population of just over 12,000 people, Sweetwater is at the Texas crossroads—far enough west to be in cattle country, but far enough south to be in the fertile oil grounds. During the heyday of the Texas oil boom in the late '70s and '80s, Sweetwater had its share of money rolling around.

It's windy, dusty, and hot in Sweetwater—not exactly the poster city for the Texas Department of Tourism. Perfect, though, for oil country, cattle farming, or a John Wayne movie (it still burns me up that the Duke was born in Iowa and not Texas). It sits below the Texas caprock, but it's pretty flat.

A traffic jam is a couple of cars at a stoplight. We're famous for one of the world's largest gypsum plants and the annual Rattlesnake Roundup.

At the Roundup, kids take a burlap sack and tongs and, well,

Textbook pass blocking, Homecoming 1988, ACU vs. Eastern New Mexico. We won, they lost.

round up rattlesnakes. The area Jaycees pay a certain amount per pound for the snakes. If you gather enough snakes, the Roundup can be a pretty profitable undertaking for a fifteen-year-old.

There is nothing like climbing a rocky, rolling West Texas hill, pouring butane into a hole, and hearing a whole den of rattle-snakes let you know they don't like that. They will come out shortly thereafter. That's when you grab them.

Sweetwater doesn't have the humidity of Dallas and Fort Worth because it's at a much higher elevation. In fact, you get much better gas mileage driving from Sweetwater to Dallas than you do driving from Dallas to Sweetwater.

There's your first piece of financial advice. Never leave Sweetwater after you get there. You get much better gas mileage by hanging around.

Legend precedes Texas high school football. Any story you've heard or any stereotype you have about our game is likely true. Football stars are Friday-night heroes. Kids in this part of West Texas grow up wanting to be like the local high school stars. Sweetwater was one of the capitals of West Texas football.

Not liking football in Sweetwater would be like not liking the Catholic church if you lived in the Vatican. Everything revolved around our team and our upcoming event, in season or not. The school didn't allow spring baseball because officials thought it would interfere with the football off-season. No wrestling, because it might interfere with the football off-season. Even if you ran track or played basketball, you still went through football off-season. In Texas high school, there are basically two sports: football and off-season football.

We thought football was so important that we had an indoor practice facility (remember, this is in the early 1980s). We didn't need it to protect us from the weather. We needed it to prevent other area coaches finding out that we were practicing in there creatively. I say *creatively* because my hometown wouldn't do anything illegal. You see, it was against UIL rules to scrimmage during the spring; however, if you had an indoor practice facility you could do this without getting caught because you could close and lock the doors.

This facility was nicer than anything at any college in West Texas. The oil money had gotten to be so big around this time that the oilmen just spent it on whatever they wanted. They wanted Sweetwater to remain atop the Texas football heap, so they pooled some money and built this thing. We also had one of the nicest stadiums in the state. The stadium was a bowl. We had the latest and greatest surface, bleachers, benches, and scoreboard. You name it, we had it.

At the time, we had about 12,000 people in town, and we would draw 8,000 or more for our home play-off games. When we played out of town or in the play-offs, almost all the stores in town shut down. People would line the highways up to fifty miles away from where we were playing with banners on fences, so we would see all these signs while driving. You can understand why I had a hard time giving up my dream of keeping on playing football. It was a great place to grow up.

Life just stopped on Friday night everywhere in town because football was the king. Football was the commodity, and the coaches were the power brokers.

Texas high school football coaches can make up to six figures. A lot of coaches in West Texas made great money when I was in school in the mid- to late '80s because the oil was flowing. Coaches would get their regular salary and then, likely, a huge bonus for doing a little Saturday-morning football talk show on radio. Normally a bunch of businessmen got together to pay the coach just to keep him in town and away from rival high schools. These shows were a lot like what you see college coaches building into their contracts these days. He might make $50,000 for his coaching job, but he could make upward of double that if had a successful show. In Sweetwater, that was certainly the case.

In Texas, there are five classifications under the University Interscholastic League. The small schools are in Class A, the ones a little larger in 2A, and so on until you get to the Class 5A schools, the ones in Dallas, Houston, San Antonio, and some of the larger towns that might have only one or two high schools.

Sweetwater was in Class 4A during my run from 1981 to 1985. We stayed 4A because, for the most part, we creatively created a few extra students so we could stay 4A. Most schools would like to go down in class so they could be more competitive. Sweetwater had a tremendous amount of pride that we were 4A, and we wanted to stay that way. It normally meant generating a few more students, but that didn't matter. We could always make a few more students show up on the day the numbers were counted, even if they really didn't show up. This often made us one of the smallest 4As in the state. In the play-offs, we'd often play schools twice our size as far as enrollment.

With my mom outside of Sweetwater High School gym, the day she won fan of the year.

The town was 12,000, but the county was only 16,000. Basically, the county consisted of Sweetwater and another town, Roscoe. There was no competition for entertainment. Dallas was four hours away, Midland/Odessa the same. No major entertainment groups ever went there. There weren't any major league sports. Really, all people had year-round, as in most towns in West Texas, was their football program and girls' basketball. However, they wouldn't let the guys play with the girls (at least on the basketball court), so the only option was to play football.

Oil Money and Football—The Good Ol' Days

Here's how much people thought about the game: These oil companies would catch wind of a star athlete somewhere. It didn't even have to be in Texas. Then the companies would recruit kids to different high schools by offering their parents a job. They came to work for the company, and Junior went to the high school and became a star.

It was a fun place to grow up, especially if you were a football player. If you were a male tennis player, it probably wasn't the place you wanted to be.

Working on my brother-in-law's ranch, outside of Sweetwater.

Hauling Hay with Illegal Aliens

I wanted to be a part of this badly. I wanted to be the one kids emulated. The summer between my freshman and sophomore year I worked for my brother-in-law, Butch Sims. I hauled hay almost every day in the one-hundred-degree heat. Hay can be baled two ways: where a tractor picks it up or where you pick it up. Butch went the route of producing smaller bales and then having us load them onto the truck, take them to the barn, and unload them there. I don't think it ever occurred to him to build the barn closer to the hay.

I think mainly he chose the small bales because he was paying me next to nothing, and the other two gentlemen who worked with me, Benito and Cristino (who I don't think were legal residents of our fine state or country), didn't make much either.

We had a several-person crew each day that would pick the bales up from the ground and put them on a flatbed truck. While other guys I worked with would only get one to two bales on the truck in a certain distance, I tried to get double or triple what they got. I wasn't just hauling hay, I was getting ready for football season.

I even stuck weights in my cowboy boots and would do as much running as I could. I would grab a bale on one side of the truck, run to the other side, get another bale on, and then back to the other side.

I would run behind the tractor back to the barn. I think Benito and Cristino thought I was a loco American.

My junior year I started to come into my own. I was now six-four, but still only 175 pounds. I could play on the line. I still wasn't very fast, but I was getting stronger and learning the game. Actually, the thing I learned was that if you wanted to play bad enough, the coach would find a place to put you.

The hard work was beginning to pay off. I began to get all sorts of honors. I had a good junior season and was first team All-State my senior year. They even had a compilation team of all the divisions, and I made first team on this one as well. I was living the dreams and goals I had set for myself years before.

It looked like working as hard as I did those few years was

about to make the first part of that dream come true, playing football at Abilene Christian University.

It may seem strange that I would have going to Abilene Christian and playing football there as one of my life goals, but not when you realize where and how I grew up.

I had grown up going to Abilene Christian football games. I grew up idolizing their players. I was now going to be one of their players. I had grown up looking at the All-American pictures that hung around their basketball coliseum, Moody Coliseum. I wanted my picture to hang up there with the Feasel brothers, Wilbert Montgomery, and gold medalist Bobby Morrow. My picture hung up in the field house at Sweetwater, and I wanted it in Moody Coliseum as well. It was the first of my three goals, and it was about to be crossed off the list.

My father, Lavelle Layfield, was on the board of trustees. A lot of my relatives had gone there. It was the next logical move for me.

It wasn't the smartest move careerwise. The smartest thing to do would have been to go the University of Texas and play football.

Because I had never really been outside of Sweetwater, the University of Texas might as well have been the University of Washington to me. Every day when I picked up the paper, I saw something about Abilene Christian.

I did take some of the recruiting trips, simply because they were offered. None of it made a dent in my desire to go to ACU. I committed early, which cost me a Southwest Conference scholarship. It didn't really matter.

Looking back, it would have been smarter to go somewhere else to play football because you have a bigger platform and better competition. But I didn't have anything to complain about. I was about to achieve lifelong goal number 1, and I was going to do it in a place that I held sacred.

My father, mom, sister, and brother had all gone there. However, my brother, Paul, would be the only Layfield that would get into more trouble than me. He had to finish at Texas A and M.

It was like a natural progression for me, a progression I didn't fight because of the adulation I had for the school. I think my parents thought I would be doomed for eternity if I didn't go to Abilene Christian University. I wanted to go too, so I didn't mind the pressure.

ACU Homecoming 1976— Greatest Recruiting Day Ever

I remember one Saturday in 1976 we were in Abilene watching ACU play a homecoming football game. Ove Johansson lined up for a 69-yard field goal. I scampered to the end zone with my cousin Alan Rich and the rest of the kids to try to catch the ball after it went through the uprights. Ove made the try with plenty to spare, the longest field goal ever recorded.

That same day, Wilbert Montgomery, who went on to play for the Philadelphia Eagles, broke the NAIA-II rushing all-time touchdown record.

I followed closely when Billy Olson was breaking pole-vault world records. Abilene Christian was the ultimate for me, and I intended to set my mark there as well.

When I finally got on campus, I realized another challenge was being thrown in my face. While I enjoyed being at ACU, they didn't always enjoy me.

ACU is a private school affiliated with the Church of Christ. Because it is privately funded, the administrators can make their own rules. I joke a lot and like to kid around, but what you're about to read is real. There is actually a place that existed, and still exists, that operates this way. I went to ACU in the fall of '85. It may as well have been the fall of 1885.

Now please understand, I really liked ACU, it was just that the rules were a little off the chart on the conservative side. However, I have good memories there, which do outweigh the few bad ones. And while I truly don't like a few people there to this day, there were many, many more that I learned to love.

Is This a College or an Amish Colony?

When I was at ACU, no shorts were allowed on campus. I believe that rule has been modified, but at this time you could only wear shorts in athletic areas for athletic events. There was mandatory daily chapel. Monday through Friday, you were expected to attend chapel services. Actually, you weren't expected to attend—you had to attend. Roll was taken, and you could be suspended if you didn't go. At first they assigned seats for all 4,000 students, then they installed electronic machines where you had to punch in to be counted. I think somehow you lose the value of a church service when you have to punch in electronically. Needless to say, I found a way around this.

Probably the hardest rule for me to follow during my ACU days was their prohibition policy. If you were enrolled at ACU or drew a paycheck from the school, you could not go to any place where the primary purpose was to drink alcohol or dance. Restaurants like Chili's, for example, that served alcohol were fine because their primary purpose wasn't to serve alcohol. The bottom line was that even if you were thirty-eight years old and were a professional student enrolled at ACU, you couldn't have a drink.

Abilene Christian believed it to be un-Christian to indulge in alcoholic beverages. I believed it un-American not to. I am just glad that when Jesus turned the water into wine, He and the apostles were not enrolled at ACU. He would have had to turn the wine back to water, or else they would have been suspended if they had a drink.

There were always stories about teachers going out and ordering a mixed drink in a coffee cup so they could have a cocktail with their meal. If they were caught drinking, they would have been fired. (Now don't any of you teachers worry. Even though I know who you are, I won't tell on you here.)

Is That the Dean in the Bushes?

Because of Abilene's relatively small size, there were only a few bars in town. The ACU administration knew them well. So did I. Actually, they just knew the landscaping well. Administrators would—once again you just have to keep reading and believing—go to the bars and hide in the bushes or sneak around to see if they could see ACU stickers on cars parked at the bars. These people would actually troll for beer drinkers. They would take down a license plate number and then run the plate when they got back to the school to see if it matched any registered to an ACU student.

My college roommates, John Buesing and Mark McIntyre, and me. My dad is in the background.

I probably should have told them to put me on probation and I would take the standard punishment, because I was going to have a hard time following this policy. I am just glad they didn't believe in caning people at the GATA fountain, the center of the school. Now understand that just as you cannot blame the Crusades and the Holy Wars and all the bad things on Christianity, you can't blame some of the zealots that were bona fide idiots on ACU.

Sweetwater looked a little differently on drinking. It wasn't as taboo there. If you had a beer in Sweetwater, you were just being one of the boys. If you tipped one up at ACU, you were headed to hell.

My age and curiosity and my enrollment at ACU were about to mix like oil and water. It was only a matter of time before something happened.

My first year at ACU, I got in trouble. It didn't exactly take a team from the NASA station in Houston to predict this was going to happen. For some, the rules, and forty-five-year-old men hiding in bushes outside a bar checking license plates, had no effect. They took something away from me that I wanted to do.

I wanted to sit down with a beer and watch a football game, but I wasn't allowed. The rules created a fantasy world. You had a lot of kids who had never seen anything other than this fantasy world. They had been in private schools since they started school. Now they were in yet another private school that was doing nothing more than sheltering them from the real world. I do think these rules were well intended, just misapplied.

I never did anything illegal. Had I been at a state school, I would have been doing nothing more than any other normal student was doing. But since I was six-foot-seven, a football player, and a high-profile recruit from a nearby town, I stuck out. A normal student could likely walk into a bar, tilt a glass, and walk away untouched. If I walked into that same bar and picked up that same glass, someone was going to recognize me—that is, if the dean and his camouflaged friends didn't do it first.

My freshman year I was at a get-together that was indeed serving adult beverages; however, the drinking age was nineteen at the time, and I was nineteen. The phone rang, and I noticed no one was answering it. I picked it up. It was my RA. He recognized my voice. I can only imagine what was happening to him on the other end of the line. He asked me if I was at the party. Now realize this: He actually asked me if I was there. Wow. I'm not even going to touch the stupidity on this one. I answered that I was at the party. He asked if I was drinking. I also answered in the affirmative. Hey, we were into morals at ACU, and I was doing my part. I was telling the truth. I was drinking. My honesty didn't help me much when the dean found out.

The second time I got into trouble was a few years later at my college roommate's house. John Buesing, who is now a Texas state trooper in the Fort Worth area, was planning a big twenty-second birthday party. I was to be there with my party hat on. No problem. If we saw someone, we invited him or her. It was going to be the bash to end all Abilene bashes. John was a couple years older than me and was about to graduate. I felt it was my duty to send my man off in the right way. The guys understand.

We had the party. And I mean, we had *the* party.

We certainly sent John out the way any man would want to be sent out. Now would be a good time to talk about the typical girl at ACU, because she is about to play a big role in my battle with ACU administration. There were a group of girls we called "bowheads" because they always wore bows in their hair. They dressed like Laura Ingalls Wilder from *Little House on the Prairie*. Bows in their hair, and eyes on trying to find a rich husband. They acted like the greatest saints in the world in order to fool a young man whose parents were rich into marrying them.

There were all kinds of bowheads at John's party. At the party, they didn't have the bows in their hair. Probably didn't have both feet on the floor either, as according to dorm rules. Maybe both feet pointed toward the ceiling, but probably not on the floor. Two of these bowheads were called into a disciplinary session the next day. A plea bargain was offered. Stooge on the big guys and your sentence will be light, was the delivered message. The names "John Layfield" and "John Buesing" were music to ACU's ears. A donor could have called and said, "I feel like donating five million dollars next week," and the dean wouldn't have been happier than he was after hearing our names.

Counsel the Grown Men
Hiding in the Bushes . . . Not Me

We didn't get expelled, but I wish we had been. Instead, we were ordered to attend an alcoholic counseling session and visit with a psychologist. John and I were slapped with community service and ordered to write a book report on the dangerous effects of gateway drugs. We were also handed a 566-question test to determine our mental stability. The questions were great: Are you afraid of spiders? Have you ever thought about beating anybody up?

I could deal with the rest of the punishment. The counseling session, though, was a bit much.

We walked into the session together to find the biggest geek I had ever seen standing in front of the room, leading the session. I'm not a big fan of the counseling profession. I think this guy got a job as a counselor because he couldn't associate with anything else in life.

He started the session by making us go around the room and tell why we were there. It turned into one big lying session.

One girl would say, "I just had one margarita." Another would say, "I just had one beer." The counselor got around to John first. John wasted no time.

"What are you here for?" the counselor asked. "What did you have to drink?"

"Well," John said, "it was my twenty-second birthday, and I had about thirty beers. One for each year and then a few more."

I confirmed to the counselor that, indeed, John had gone a case plus a six-pack. Jaws dropped; according to that counselor, he had just witnessed Satan and hedonism walking side by side into his precious session.

The incident, though, left a sour taste in the dean's mouth as well as the mouth of our athletic director.

Now understand that there were a couple of athletic directors and deans while I was at school. The first dean I had was Norman Archibald, who, though he had had to discipline me, I respected and liked—as did everyone. The first athletic director, Wally Bullington, was a good man as well.

The Dynamic Duo

The second athletic director inherited a great athletic program. He would leave it in shambles. He was without a doubt the worst thing that ever happened to ACU athletics.

The second dean, I believe, just couldn't find a job anywhere else.

This dynamic duo determined that the events I had been involved in during my three years at ACU were too much for them to handle. They decided that my football scholarship was no longer valid. They stripped me of my financial aid. I had made several All-America teams my junior year. Now, I was a returning All-American that was about to walk onto the ACU team.

I want to repeat that. I made second team All-American as a junior and had to *pay* to come back to school.

I'm not saying I was never at fault in any of these events. I was an eager college kid having a good time. I did break the school rules, though I never did anything illegal. Believe me, ACU was not to blame; the only problem I had that wasn't my fault was with a couple of men who held positions that unfortunately affected me directly. I believe they loved affecting me very much.

I was doing a lot for the university on the field. In fact, through all my troubles with the administration and the dynamic duo, football was my escape. It was the one place where I was able to be myself. I didn't have to worry about Dean Rambo in the bushes or anyone making plea bargains to send me to counseling sessions.

I would have to say, though, that one of the worst incidents of getting into trouble, certainly the oddest, was partly our athletic director's fault. He just didn't understand the rules.

My coach in college was John Payne. Coach Payne coached with Washington in the NFL and was a pleasure to play for. I can't tell you how hard it is to write that someone who used to help beat my beloved Dallas Cowboys is a great man. He was good to me, and we always got along. I loved his tough, hard-nosed style, and he respected how hard I played the game. Coach Payne wanted tough players. He never understood why the young players he brought in weren't as tough and willing as he was.

Good Devotionals . . . Bad Football Games

My junior year we were coming off an off-season of changes. The athletic director decided that Coach Payne needed to recruit more good old-fashioned church players. The decision left Coach Payne with some nice young Church of Christ men. It made for fantastic devotionals.

It also produced a bunch of young men that weren't exactly football-acclimated. To put it nicely.

In fact, I remember one day we got a recruit in that had a broken jaw. They claimed this showed he was a fighter; my argument was, we should recruit the guy who broke his jaw. We kept getting the guys who lost.

Because there was a lack of fire (which is a nice way of saying we had recruited a bunch of sissies), Coach Payne gathered us around every day at the beginning of practice for the "Bull in the Ring" drill. This drill is pretty self-explanatory. One guy stands in the middle of a circle, and one by one, guys come at him from all direction, trying to knock him out of the ring.

The drill had good intentions. But if dogs don't bite when they're pups, they aren't going to bite when they are dogs. In other words, if a nineteen-year-old guy isn't tough already, you're not making him tough all of the sudden with one drill.

In "Bull in the Ring" everything was legal—for the most part. Kicking, punching, whatever it took to throw a guy out of the ring. I never had a guy throw me out.

Wrestling an 800-Pound Brown Bear

One day some freshmen approached me after practice.

"Hey, how do you think you would do against a bear?" one asked.

"A bear?" I asked, trying to remember a story I thought I had heard about legendary Alabama coach Paul "Bear" Bryant getting his name from wrestling a bear. "I would beat him. That's how I would do."

I had forgotten about this conversation before I had my pads off that day. The freshmen had not. About a month later, the same freshman told me that the bear was in town.

"What bear?" I asked.

"The bear you're going to wrestle," he said.

So now I've got a problem. Do I back down and look like a liar? Or do I go down to the bar and wrestle this thing? At this point, I was thinking this bear couldn't be any more than 300 pounds at the most. I was about 280 at the time, so I thought even though I was a little undersized, I could outthink this thing.

The bear I was to wrestle was at a local cowboy bar named Butterfield Junction.

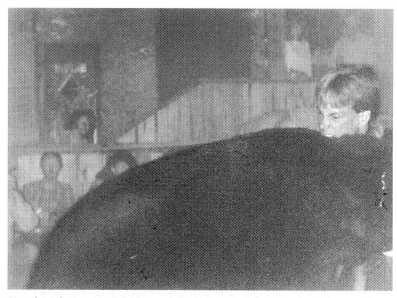

You thought it was a tale. Me and the bear in the bar (the bear is the brunette). This didn't last long.

I headed down to Butterfield Junction, a little country bar in Abilene. John Buesing went with me and promised to wrestle the thing first. For those of you that don't know what a cowboy/country bar is, here's a brief "Cowboy Bars for Dummies" lesson. Go to your garage and saw up every piece of wood in the place. Leave the sawdust on the floor. Take a bag of peanuts, eat the whole bag, and throw the shells on the floor. Now prop up a couple of stools next to a long piece of wood that is about five feet off the floor. That's your bar. Now get a bunch of neon signs with the state of Texas outlined and the Bud Light logo inside. Throw in a bunch of Wrangler jeans that look like they have been spray-painted on with blue Krylon, rows of Stetson hats (straw after Easter and before Labor Day, black felt the rest of the year), and boots made from every animal that has skin to peel. You've got Butterfield Junction.

John and I got out of the car with only dollar signs on our mind. If one of us got the bear on his back, $1,500 was headed that man's way.

I already had plans for the money. If I won, I was going to consider that gainful employment outside the semester.

Well, not really. I was going to put the $1,500 in my pocket and lie about it. Those plans were far down the road. One big obstacle was between the moolah and me. I just didn't know how big the obstacle was.

When John and I got closer to the door, we saw a picture of this huge bear. I pointed the picture out to my cheering section/bloodthirsty teammates and laughed. This had to be hype, I thought. No way was a bear that big going to walk out on that floor. That picture, once again I thought, was just there to draw people inside.

I was wrong.

John went first. The bear that walked out to face John was over eight feet tall and weighed over 800 pounds. Now John is a very tough and very big man, but the bear didn't seem very impressed. Poor John.

This bear didn't just walk out onto the floor. In wrestling, we have our entrance themes. The themes normally, if this makes sense, sound like the wrestler or team's personality. At least, that's the goal.

This bear had his own theme. With rock music blaring all over this place, the bear was led to the ring like he was Mike Tyson. In between gasps, I thought: He's an 800-pound bear. He doesn't need music.

His head was as big as a stop sign. The trainers had choke chains to keep things in control. His front teeth were also taken out so he couldn't eat human flesh. After seeing John lose rather decisively, I decided there was no way I was getting out there.

"You've got to do it," the freshmen reminded me.

What was I going to do? I was a team leader. I had to show these guys what it meant to be tough. So, with my gym shorts and tennis shoes on, I walked out to the center of the dance floor.

I got out there with this stinking bear. And he did stink. He slobbered all over me. Because he didn't have any front teeth, he chewed all the skin off my neck and one of my ears with his gums. This bear wasn't only huge, he also knew how to use his body. He swung his paws like they were baseball mitts. He just pawed me to death. His claws had been removed, but the swats were more like Joe Frazier left hooks, claws or no claws.

I want to set the record straight quickly. I know that I'm wrestling this thing on the dance floor. This wasn't the first time I've rolled around the dance floor with a big, hair, stinky thing. I figure I've got the home-field advantage. It was the first time, however, I'd ever had to sign a waiver saying I wouldn't sue if I were killed as a result of rolling around with a big, hairy, sweaty thing on a dance floor.

A few seconds into the match, I realized the bear was wrestling as hard as I was. That was the way he'd been trained. When I started to back down a little, he thought I wanted to play. When he relaxed, I threw him on his side.

Memo to anyone who wrestles a bear: Don't make him mad. Play dead, anything, but don't make him mad.

The bear erupted. He made the most God-awful snort I ever heard in my life. I've never heard anything like this before and never want to again. It was piercing. He shot up and threw me across the whole dance floor.

There was a rug on the floor, but that did more damage than good. The bear slung me under a table. I was trapped. Butterfield Junction was packed. I had nowhere to go, and 800 pounds of ticked-off Smokey headed my direction. Under the table, a thought crossed my mind: You might see this on the Discovery Channel or in *National Geographic,* but not in a cowboy bar.

Now, I've been charged in cowboy bars before, but never by something as mad as this thing. The bear reached me and decided his paws hadn't had enough. He swatted until he got his fill. Actually, it was until the trainers had seen enough. It took two trainers to pull me out from underneath him and a stiff steel rod to the head to get him to quit attacking. I felt like kissing those two trainers. This bear had completely lost his temper. He was trying to kill me.

Of course, my cheering section/bloodthirsty teammates and the rest of the place were going wild. They were seeing a guy getting mauled by a brown bear. They thought it was fantastic. The treat of a lifetime. A little under five minutes after I started wrestling, I was beaten. I was just glad it wasn't brown bear mating season.

The next day, I woke up sore, bruised, ear almost eaten off, and invited to a meeting with the athletic director. I had been in trouble several times already, and I had always told the truth, and it never helped me, so this time I looked him straight in the eye and lied. I told him that I had done a lot of foolish things in my life, but I wouldn't do anything as dumb as wrestling a bear.

You might say I had problems with animals in college—the bear that mauled me and the jackass I had for an athletic director. When he found out the truth, he wasn't as upset that I had wrestled the bear as that I was at Butterfield Junction at all. I had almost been mauled by a brown bear, and the donkey man was more worried that my life would be ruined because I was at a bar. Butterfield Junction was one of those places where drinking was the primary purpose. Remember those ACU no-nos? Going to Butterfield Junction was one of them. A number of ACU students were there that night, drinking, dancing, and watching the bear ravage me. That wasn't the reason *I* was there. *I* was there to bear-wrestle, which is not covered in the ACU no-nos. It wasn't in the book, so I couldn't be punished. The donkey man felt otherwise, and disciplinary action was once again headed my way.

Looking back at it, if I had known the bear was almost going to kill me, I would have used the bar for its primary purpose. I would not only have broken the rules, I would have shattered them.

Not long after my last season, in which I *did* pay to go to school and *did* make consensus All-American, I got the greatest phone call of my life. I was going to Los Angeles to play with the silver and black—the Raiders. Talk about a perfect fit.

The day the Raiders called, I crossed off goal number 2, Play Pro Football, and figured goal number 3, Get Rich, would follow.

Country Boy Goes to the City

Sure enough, it did—at least by my standards. When the Raiders told me I was getting a $5,500 signing bonus, I spent like I was Bill Gates.

Remember, I'm from Sweetwater, Texas. I thought goal number 3 had been accomplished. I took the pickup down to the stereo shop and got the loudest thing I could get. Then I just took off. I took off toward Los Angeles with not so much as a plan in mind. I stopped in Fort Sumner, New Mexico, so I could see Billy the Kid's grave. I took a detour to Las Vegas simply because I had never been there. I was such a big spender that I sat down at the $5 blackjack tables. I was a serious spender now.

The day after Vegas, I wheeled the pickup truck into the Raiders complex in El Segundo, right next to the brand-new BMW that belonged to all-pro defensive end Lyle Alzado. I went into the complex and almost immediately got my check. All I had to do was sign my name. After getting that check, I wanted to sign my name about five hundred times. They showed me to my locker, which was right by Bob Golic's and catty-corner to Howie Long's.

I spent every dime of my $5,500 signing bonus. I think it took three months. Some athletes have gone through money quicker, but I didn't have a drug problem. Mine was basically spent on having a great time. That was in 1989, when the dollar went a little further. I didn't live lavishly as far as fancy hotels or outrageous partying. I went out every night if I wanted, ate where I wanted to. I was the ultimate tourist. I did everything there was to do in Los Angeles. You name a tourist attraction, and I did it. They were minor things, but I was certainly blowing my money.

You make a lot of important decisions when you are young. Some are made when you aren't really mature enough to understand all your options. One of the major problems I had is similar to the obstacle young couples face when they are starting out. They see how much wealth their parents or other older people have accumulated. They start comparing themselves to what these older people have, without factoring in the number of years their elders have spent building this wealth.

I saw the Marcus Allens, Howie Longs, and Lyle Alzados of the world and how much they had. I knew I couldn't spend like they could, but I tried to keep up on a smaller level. Fast-forward almost three years later, and I was in no better position financially than I had been when I started. I had a lot more stories, but not any more money.

Thankfully, I realized my necessity. I had reached two of my three goals, but—when I was cut by the Raiders—I was back to square one in a sense. I had no money, no job, and little direction.

I had spent my life getting ready for a career in football. Now that was over. The problem was, I was still young, and I only had enough money to refill my gas tank once, not to retire. I had gotten the opportunity to do many things that were quite literally a dream come true. I was not bitter about my fate in life, I was happy I had gotten the chance to do the things I had done. The only thing I regretted was how I had handled my money, which was very poorly. I would dedicate the next part of my life to learning everything I could about money and investing so that this wouldn't happen again.

I was very lucky that I got a second chance at an early age. Very few people get a second chance.

I want to help you through what has happened to me. Whether you need a second chance or just want a better future, I promise you I can help. My life experience has been a great teacher for me, and it can be for you too. You can learn through my mistakes and through my successes.

No great truth of financial management was ever revealed to me. I simply learned through experience the truths that are important to a normal person trying to get out of debt.

It really is a pretty easy process. Remember, I didn't say painless.

Take my drive from San Antonio to Athens. I could have learned a couple of ways to make the trip. I could have looked at a map or just started driving down the road. Both methods would have eventually led me to Athens. But until I drove the route for the first time, I wouldn't have known the road.

When I was at ACU, I had a hard time understanding how someone who was teaching, for example, Public Speaking 101 could teach about public speaking without having actually gone out and done public speaking. It's like looking at a map. You can look at the drive on the map, visualize what it looks like, and plan a route. But until you have been down the exact road, you don't know what it looks like on the route or what obstacles are on the roads.

This is why I can help you on your way to financial freedom. A lot of people can lay the theories out and read you directions; I have seen the orange construction cones on the road. I smell like smoke because I have been in the fire so much and so long. I know what it feels like to be broke. I know what it feels like to have to begin completely anew. I have been there, and I have found a way to climb out of that hole. This is what I want to help you do. No matter how deep you are in that hole, whether a little or so far down that your voice echoes, everyone can use a little help. There are some out there that think they can tell you what it's like. Fact is, most of these people have never had to climb out themselves. I have a proven way that I know works.

I've been through the financial fires. I've fought the battles. I've got the scars. I have been down to $27, a blue pickup running low on gas, and a stinking quote from Ben Franklin; and I made a tremendous comeback. I can help you by sharing my experiences, my mistakes, and what I've learned to do and not to do. When your financial future is settled, or at least on the right track, your peace of mind will be greatly improved. I got a second chance to have that peace. Read on, and I will help you have it too.

Summary

- **Being poor ain't fun; staying that way is stupid.**

- **Wrestle brown bears in bars only when it is not mating season.**

CHAPTER | 1

PLAY THE HAND DEALT YOU

Life Goes On

The great poet Robert Frost said he could sum up everything he's learned about life in three words: It goes on.

Only when you realize that the past cannot be changed and only the future remains will you be able to plan that future. It is very easy to know where you want to be, but if you don't know where you are, then you will have an extremely hard time planning a route to get there.

There are counseling offices around the world full of people that want to blame the system for their circumstances. The sun was in their eyes, their shoes were untied, or—ever popular— their environment was not conducive to success. For goodness' sake, if Abilene Christian University had not discriminated against me with such silly rules as attending class and making good grades, I would have graduated with honors.

Dr. Carl Jung said, "When you realize that the whole world has problems, then you are on your way to mental health."

Once you realize that you are not the only person in the world who has a mortgage and other problems, then you can figure out a way to a better future. Everyone has problems to deal with; the key to success is how you deal with those problems.

If all your time is spent thinking about how badly life has mistreated you, all your time is spent in the past and you are ignoring your future. You are gravely mistreating yourself, and there won't be any improvement in your situation. However, you can't spend your time patting yourself on the back either, which is also doing your future no good. You simply have to play the hand dealt to you.

Where you are in life, good or bad, there is nothing you can do about it. You can only control where you will be in the future.

Cindy and I outside of Sigmund Freud's office in Vienna. Lost part of my head, but no case of envy.

Sigmund Freud's Couch

I have never been to Dr. Jung's office, but I have been to the office in Vienna, Austria, of his main rival—Dr. Sigmund Freud. In 1994 I was working in Vienna for Otto Wanz and Peter William for the Catch Wrestling Association. On a day off, my wife, Cindy, and I decided to go sightseeing. Actually, we spent most of our time sightseeing; I once told Otto that this wrestling every night was really getting in the way of us seeing the world.

We decided this day to go to see Dr. Freud's preserved office. As we entered the office, I realized that we were standing in front of Dr. Freud's famous couch. It was roped off, and there was a guard there. I couldn't resist the temptation of sitting on the couch, so I waited for the guard to leave the room, then I moved past the barricade and sat on the famous couch. Nothing happened. I did sit on the couch, but the envy that Dr. Freud was so famous for talking about never materialized. If it did, I sure wouldn't admit it here.

You can spend all your time griping about the past, talking about opportunities missed, or you can spend it planning a better future. A lot of people around the world do exactly this. They gripe about where they are in life and the circumstances that got them there. They spend so much time griping about the past that their future is affected negatively by the fact they won't spend any time planning to make it better. The cards you are dealt have to be played in the best possible way. Griping about the dealer won't help you any.

My options when I was released from the World League were simple. I could gripe about bad knees and unfortunate timing, or I could go on with my life and figure out what I was going to do next. I had wasted what I made financially, though I had an extremely good time doing it. And I do mean a good time. Actually, I had a great time.

It's always fun to blow money. The problem was, I didn't find a medium where I was enjoying life and also preparing for a future. I had priced perfection into my future, something virtually everyone does. However, pricing perfection into your future can be extremely dangerous. You will see this phrase quite often in this book.

Remember, I don't believe in making yourself miserable now because you are planning for your retirement. You have to enjoy life now; there is no guarantee you will be on this earth until retirement.

Life is about living, not just existing.

However, money and opportunities are too hard to come by to waste foolishly, and I decided not to let that happen again.

Life on the Bread Line

The day I was released from the World League, I didn't have many options. I kept going on up I-35 back toward Athens, realizing that there was nothing I could change about what had happened with my career and my finances. The past was gone; there was nothing I could do to change the fact that I was broke. I had to have a plan. I had realized this at last. I guess some things have to be learned the hard way for some people—but learn I did. I knew that whatever I did, if I were fortunate enough to make decent money again, I would not blow a second chance.

I came to the realization that five years from that point, I needed to be better off than I was then, or I would have just wasted five more years. Although having $28 in my bank account would have been a little bit better, I also realized I needed to quantify how much better off I wanted to be.

It was hard admitting to myself that where I was financially was not where I should be, but I knew that was the truth. I had to come to the realization that I had not been good with my finances. It is extremely hard to admit failure. Remember, I said this was easy, not painless.

Convincing yourself of that reality is the first, and usually the hardest, step in figuring out your next move. A lot of people know where they want to be. But unless you know where you are currently, you can't plan the most direct route to get there.

I had spent three years playing professional football, and fulfilled one of my childhood dreams. I thought I would play a lot longer, but that didn't come to pass. I had always thought I would enjoy being a wrestler. I am not one of these guys who got into wrestling because I had no other options. Being a wrestler was appealing to me. I wanted to be part of this great entertainment genre.

I was a big fan at a time when Texas wrestling was in its heyday. I used to love to watch wrestling every Saturday night at ten o'clock with my grandfather, Cato Sheerer, who I thought the world of. I remember pulling for Fritz Von Erich and rooting against Skandor Akbar. Little did I know how fond I would grow of Akbar as my manager when I started out as a bad guy in Texas, and how much he would help me in the wrestling business.

I even set up a wrestling ring made of garden hose wrapped around trees, and the neighborhood kids and I would wrestle. I was the reigning champion of Hailey Street.

I actually have a past of violence in my family. I am a direct descendant of the MacGregors from Scotland, of which Rob Roy was the most famous. In fact, Rob Roy was the one that got our name banned for many years. I still plan on returning to Scotland and reclaiming my homeland one day.

Back during its heyday, wrestling was done in territories. The Von Erichs in Dallas and the Funks in Amarillo ruled Texas. These were the two wrestling shows I got to watch when I was growing up in Sweetwater. There was a World Wrestling Federation then, but it was a northeastern territory, and we didn't get any of their television programming.

Some guys could be one character in one territory and a completely different one in another territory. There were no national television deals like there are now. A wrestler may have been a good guy in Minneapolis, but when he came to Texas, he could be a bad guy and few, if any, fans knew. Television deals were syndicated locally or, at best, statewide.

Even though I was basically starting over, I looked at my situation as a chance for a second career. I had always thought football was going to be my career path. Now I was getting a chance at another dream, *and* a second chance at my financial future.

There are all kinds of stories about people breaking into the wrestling business. There is no one tried-and-true way. There's no college draft, no true farm system. You have to promote yourself and learn the hard way how to get to the top. Some make it through a certain contact. Some are second- and third-generation wrestlers. Others spend years on the independent circuit, hoping someone from WWE picks up on them or hears enough about them to give them a look. There is only a certain amount of WWE television time each week. People who make it to WWE aren't exactly happy about giving up their roster spot; they worked too long to get there. Of course, out of the many that try, most never do make it to WWE.

When I got started, options were there, but I had already defined my goal. I knew where I wanted to be. The hard part was planning the road map of how to get there. That was the first part of my route. I wanted to go to the best wrestling school around.

Right or wrong, I felt playing at a Division II college hurt me in the NFL and World League drafts. Some great players have come from smaller schools—the best receiver to ever play, Jerry Rice, went to Mississippi Valley State; Walter Payton, one of the NFL's all-time leading rushers, went to Jackson State; and Tennessee quarterback Steve McNair played at Alcorn State. There are plenty of small-school NFL success stories. But for the most part, players at that level have a mark against them.

Brad Rheingans

I got in touch with Brad Rheingans, one of the best 220-pound Greco-Roman wrestlers in our country's history. Brad finished fourth in the 1976 Montreal Olympics. He was the favorite to win gold in the 1980 Summer Games in Moscow, but the United States boycotted the games. It's amazing how something like the Olympics that is supposed to be apolitical could be used as political leverage. All the boycott did in 1980 was hurt the dreams and goals of a bunch of our young men and women who wanted so badly to represent this great country. Brad was now running a wrestling school in Minneapolis and had (and still does have) a tremendous reputation.

So I loaded up the blue truck, and this time I headed up I-35 to Minnesota. Amazing how much time I spent on that road during this part of my career. I was playing the hand that was dealt to me in the best way I knew how to play it.

I realized that the past was gone, and the only thing I had left was my future. I decided that what I wanted was to wrestle, and I knew by looking at the number of people who'd tried and not made it that wrestling was a long shot.

I had to plan my route and do everything I could to play the hand dealt to me wisely. I knew the best chance I had was to be trained by the best, and that was why I was now in Minnesota, training with Brad.

I quickly learned that wrestling was not fake. Fixed? Yes (most of the time). Fake? No. I have been in matches where there was no set outcome, and I have been in matches and seen other matches where one outcome was called and there was a double-cross. They are few and far between, but there is always that possibility, and that does help add to the mystique of wrestling.

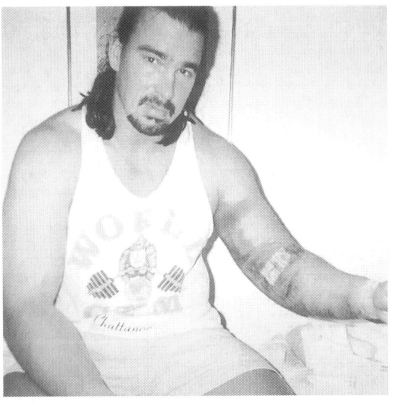

I thought wrestling was fake. My torn biceps in 2002.

"Fake" is definitely the wrong word to use. Just because you know something is coming doesn't mean it doesn't hurt.

People always ask how you learn to fall. Actually, gravity is the best teacher.

Brad was a great teacher and an even better person. I knew from the minute I got into the ring he built in his garage that this was what I wanted to do with my life. That doesn't mean it wasn't tough.

I don't think I was expecting it to be quite that tough. It was the equivalent of a very long, hard two-a-day training camp.

I loved the hard work. We would do conditioning after practice and wrestle Greco-Roman style. Brad really enjoyed doing conditioning with me. I noticed he always arranged to wrestle me; I think he enjoyed showing a former professional football player why he was a world champion. Hard work gives you a lot of pride in what you are doing. The hand I was dealt was not that great of a hand, but I was playing it as wisely as I could. I knew that this was a necessary part of going through the process of bettering myself so that I would have a chance to screw up again with my money. However, this time I knew I wouldn't blow my opportunity.

One thing you'll realize when you do finally reach your goal is that getting there can be as enjoyable as being at the top. I enjoyed the training and the discipline of Brad's wrestling school; I enjoyed the prospect of making it in the wrestling business. I truly believe that if you aren't happy now, then you won't be happy later.

Happiness is a state of mind, not a position in life.

Big Money in Independent Wrestling

It's not always going to be a lot of fun. There were times when I drove to Dallas and got $3 for driving four hours round trip by some promoter/wrestler who was taking advantage of young guys because he knew they had no option; if they didn't take the money, one of the local wrestlers would. These guys never considered the fans. I shouldn't mention any names because that would sound like sour grapes, but then again, those grapes are already sour.

I would have to say guys like Iceman King Parsons who could no longer make it to the big time were among the worst. And these guys have the audacity to wonder why you never help them when you make it. Iceman actually gave me the advice to turn down WWE and stay in local wrestling in Texas. That was sage advice; I don't know why I didn't listen. He had just generously paid me $3 for a night's work and three hours of driving.

I wondered if it was ever going to get better. I wondered if I hadn't taken a wrong turn on the road that was supposedly going to take me to WWE.

But this was my current situation. I was learning the business.

I was learning how to wrestle. I had the choice of griping about it or making the best of it. I had to play the hand dealt to me. To better yourself financially, you have to deal with your financial reality. You're not going to change what got you in your current position, so create a route to better your future. This worksheet—on the facing page—shows your current wealth state. You're still going to have to draw the future road map yourself, but this shows you where you start from.

It doesn't matter where you are—it is where you are headed that's important.
This is where you are. That number at the bottom of the worksheet may or may not look pretty, but it's reality. I once had a coach say that it didn't matter where you are, all that is important is where you are headed. That doesn't mean you have to be happy with where you are. However, you cannot plan a route to get to where you want to be until you have a starting point.

You simply have to ask yourself: Where do you want to be next year? And the next? What about five, ten, twenty years down the road? What are your goals? You don't have to have them fully defined for twenty years, but striving to improve sequentially every year needs to be the largest part of your planning.

When I first started wrestling, I got $10 for my first match. A few days later I wrestled as the main event in front of two thousand people and got $25. Sequentially I was heading the right direction; however, I was also getting screwed.

The key to being able to do what you want and to work where you want and for how long you want is to be financially independent. The way to gauge whether you are headed in the right direction is to look at your total net worth every quarter or year (something of a consistent time measure) and see that it is growing. If it is not growing, you are definitely doing something wrong. The bottom line on the worksheet is your total net worth; this is why they call it the bottom line. These financial guys are clever.

Take this sheet, look at your current state, and see exactly where you are at the present time. Do you think it has improved

NET WORTH FINANCIAL WORKSHEET

ASSETS: The Good Part

SAVINGS:	$
INVESTMENTS:	$
HOUSE VALUE:	$
VEHICLES:	$
FURNISHINGS:	$
OTHER:	$
TOTAL:	$

LIABILITIES: The Bad Part

MORTGAGE:	$
CAR LOANS:	$
OTHER LOANS:	$
CREDIT CARDS:	$
TOTAL:	$

TOTAL ASSETS:	$
-TOTAL LIABILITIES:	$
TOTAL NET WORTH:	$

*An extra copy can be found in the back of the book.

over the last few years? If not, then you have been doing something wrong. That is why I am writing this book—to help people improve their financial situations. I will give you the basics so that you can chart your own course.

The course I took worked for me, but every person is different, and each case is different. You have to have your own personal plan.

It is the same as teaching a person to fish or giving them a fish to eat. I want to teach you to fish, so that in any weather you will have fish to eat. I want to give you the cartography skills, but it will be up to you to draw your own map.

There Are No Shortcuts

Believe me when I tell you that the worst thing to do is to cut out all your bad habits at once. If you have accumulated the wrong kind of debt, and too much of it, you will have to change something. This cannot be done all at once, or it will drive you crazy. It's the same thing as having to get into good physical shape; you can't do it all at once. It is an ongoing process. All of your bad habits can't be changed at the same time.

I used to eat every day at the old B and B Café on the square in Athens, Texas, with a few good friends. My father would walk across from the First National Bank, where he worked, and meet Mutt (yes, they actually called him Mutt) Mallory, who worked next door in the First State Bank, and Coach Carl Andress—whom I had coached under for a year at Trinity Valley Community College, in between seasons in the World Football League.

Mutt was akin to a modern-day Will Rogers, and one of his favorite sayings was "If you always do what you have always done, you will always get what you have always gotten."

Sounds easy at first glance, but I believe this is one of those truisms of which it could be said, "Children could play in it but elephants could drown in it." The definition of insanity is "doing the same thing yet expecting different results."

If you keep doing the same thing, you will keep getting the same results. If the results you are getting are ideal, then congratulations, you are doing great, and I am not being facetious when I say that I am happy for you.

However, I have never met anyone who thought they had enough money. If you feel that you could be better off if you had been wiser with your money, then you will have to change something to get different results. It may not be a great change, but some change will be necessary.

Mutt was a person who understood this very well, and he tried to help others understand it also. Unfortunately, Mutt died in a hunting accident several years ago, and Coach Andress died of cancer about the same time. The world was a better place because these two men lived in it.

My father, thinking that he was spotting a trend since he was close to the same age as Coach and Mutt, decided to quit eating with me as well. So now I eat alone.

That's okay; they never let me talk anyway.

I learned a lot from being around Mutt. He believed that you could learn a lot about life through the simple things in life. You just had to look past the door, as he would say.

Golf Is Life

Playing golf to me is one of the simple things that teaches you a lesson in life—a lesson about how the past can, but shouldn't, affect the future.

I recently started playing golf again, at the invitation of my very good friend Ray Dietrich. Actually I went with him because I knew it would be fun to ride around in a cart and drink beer with him for a few hours. A golf course is the only place you can drink and drive legally. Of course, you are driving a cart on a closed course, but you have to take what you can.

I have learned to love the game.

Golf is a great teacher of life. With every hole in golf you have to learn to play the lie you have (in other words, the hand you are dealt); there is always going to be some sort of new challenge that you haven't seen. You might be behind a tree that you've never been behind before. You might not drive the ball as far as you normally do. The ball might hit a sprinkler and bounce into the rough.

Ray Dietrich and me about to play at Springhouse Golf Club in Nashville.
My slice and the beer cart were the only things working that day.

It doesn't matter where my ball lands or what new quandary I've found myself in. I still have to finish the hole. I still have to try to salvage a good score. I still have to try to save strokes.

There's a lot of strategy in this. You can't let what you just did affect how you play that second shot. If you do, your third shot will be affected, and your fourth, and your fifth, and so on.

Golf shows a person's character. You can't dwell on past success or failure. Many people believe that playing one round of golf with a person will teach you more about that person's character than a hundred meetings with them. When you are playing for a score and not just out there to have a good time, character is truly revealed. What a person will do when no one is watching truly reveals his true character. When you have a bad lie in the rough or even in the fairway, and you are absolutely certain that no one will see you improve your lie, what will you do?

My hole-in-one hole at Athens Country Club. The tree behind me is
where the ball hit; Craig Simmons, beside me, is the one I hugged.
I have no picture of the hug.

Personally, I play winter rules all year long. (Winter rules were
devised because in the winter there is not near as much grass to
hit off, and consequently you have a better chance of getting a
bad lie. Because of this, during the winter on most courses you
are allowed to improve your lie if you are in the fairway.) I figure
it has to be winter somewhere. But then again, I don't play for
score either. I believe that situations reveal character rather than
building it.

Golf reveals character. This is one of the reasons I like it so
much. Every round you play, you get the opportunity to see how
you handle every emotion that a human has. You get the chance
to handle success and failure at virtually every hole. You get to
see every round how well you respond to pressure. But the
greatest lesson you can take is that no matter what has happened, you still have to finish the hole.

Just as in life, no matter where you end up on the course and no matter what helped you to get there, you have to finish in the best way possible. You simply have to play the lie in the best way. You could be playing great and some fluke could happen, and you end up in a bad position for your next shot. The thing that you can't change, at least legally, is where you are. The only option you have is to figure out the best way to finish the hole. You can't let the past negatively affect your future.

The exact opposite could be true as well. You could be playing badly, but all the luck in the world is on your side, and despite a bad shot off the tee you end up in the middle of the fairway. The key is to remember that no matter what has happened before, you have to finish the hole.

Just finishing at Pebble Beach before going to the 19th hole with Jonathan Coachman, Patrick Murphy, and others. I beat Coach badly.

A lot of people let one or two bad shots ruin their round. They will get so upset about the fact that they have made a bad shot or chosen the wrong club that it will hurt them for the rest of the round.

Life is exactly like this. No matter where you are—it doesn't matter how you got there—you can't change the events that got you to the place where you are in life. The past is gone; the only thing that you can control is where you are headed. Wherever you are, whether it is good or bad, you have to plan your next shot. You have to decide that if where you are now is not where you think you should be, and then you have to change something.

Take a look at that financial worksheet again.

This is where you are now. It doesn't matter if you are sitting in the middle of the financial fairway with a clear shot to the hole or if you're in the financial rough. You can't control why you are where you are; you simply have to finish the hole.

In life you can't let a couple of bad shots affect you for the rest of your life, or even for the next few years. You have to learn that whatever has happened in the past is gone; the only thing you have is the future. You have to plan a route for a better future.

The past is always the past—you cannot change it. The future is not set in stone—you can make it what you want it to be.

Ron Simmons

Anyone that has seen me on WWE TV over the last few years knows my APA tag team partner, Ron Simmons. Someone recently asked me to briefly describe Ron. I told them to go look up the word *man* in the dictionary, and if Ron Simmons's picture wasn't beside the definition, then that dictionary needed to be tossed.

Ron is my tag team partner, traveling partner, and best friend. He has stepped in for me numerous times, in and out of the workplace.

In fact, we were in a bar one night shooting pool when I got into a scuffle with one of the guys next to us. Turned out he had a whole bunch of friends, and the two guys I was with, Ron and Mick Foley, were not near me. Ron, seeing that I was about to be handed a very bad loss in a barroom fight, came rushing across the bar to help.

Now understand, we were still very badly outnumbered. Ron

was voluntarily walking into a losing fight. Talk about a true friend, and a real man.

Ron grabbed a beer bottle off the nearest table and told them that he was going to hit the first man that moved. This was a little upsetting to me, because that was my gender. I was very much put at ease when Ron told me the statement didn't apply to me. I was safe to move, which I was glad of, especially since they couldn't figure who was going to eat the bottle. They left us alone.

In our business, respect is hard to come by. You earn it by knowing how to handle yourself in difficult situations. My respect for Ron knows no bounds. He knows his way around the ring and the politics of wrestling as well as anyone. He is what is good about our business.

I just have a good time when I'm with Ron. We both love to tell stories, and Ron is probably the best storyteller I know. We're like the old men that sit around and tell people stories for entertainment.

Ron grew up in Warner-Robbins, Georgia, without any parental influence. Instead of talking about environment and lack of a parental influence, he chose to make something great of himself. He developed a great work ethic that complemented a tremendous amount of God-given talent. Ron chose to play the hand dealt to him, and play it well he did. He became one of the greatest college football players of all time. Recently, I saw a quote from Florida State coach Bobby Bowden, who coached Ron in college. (Remember, Bowden has an 18-6-1 record for bowl game wins.) Bowden called Ron "the greatest player I ever coached." This from a coach that had Deion Sanders. At Florida State, Ron, along with Deion and Charlie Ward, is revered. Ron, Deion, and Charlie Ward are the only players to have had their jerseys retired.

Ron took the hand he was dealt and became a successful athlete and businessman with a great family. With the environment he grew up in, he easily could have become another thug. Ron chose to be successful, not make excuses. I am glad Ron chose to succeed, because if he didn't, he wouldn't have become the first black wrestling heavyweight champion or, more importantly, a cigar-smoking, beer-drinking APA member.

ACU vs. FSU

Now understand, Ron was one of the greatest college football players of all time, and I am very glad I never had to play against anyone that good. Also, Florida State would crush Abilene Christian quite easily now. However, this wasn't always the case. On September 25, 1954, Abilene Christian beat Florida State, 13-0, in Tallahassee. Hey, ACU doesn't have that many bragging rights for big-time football. I had to put that here.

Excuses are easy to make, it's basically saying that you are going to accept failure because you feel the world was unfair to you. There will always be things you can't control, so control what you can, the rest don't worry about.

In order to get control, look at your debt. You can control your debt by not incurring debt. Look at the financial hand you have been dealt. Now ask yourself, How will it be different in a couple of years, or five or ten years? How has it changed over the last five to ten years?

That's why you have to develop those good habits and start marking up your road map. Where you are now is important, but not as critical as where you're going. Remember the golf shot. The drive doesn't matter when you're getting ready to hit that second shot. You can't control that current spot, mentally, physically, or financially. It's part of your past. It doesn't matter how you've gotten to where you've gotten. You've got to hit that second shot. Excuses don't matter. You have to finish the hole.

Mafia Man and Buddy Landell

In 1992 and 1993 when I was making those every-six-weeks runs to Japan, trying to better myself enough to make it in the wrestling business, there were always a few wrestlers making the rounds with me, wrestlers that were brought in for just a tour or so here or there. Buddy Landell was one of these guys.

We've all heard the phrase, "You can take the boy out of the country, but you can't take the country out of the boy." That was Buddy.

When most people hear the name "Nature Boy," the tendency

is to think of the legendary Ric Flair. Buddy, who is from Tennessee, was the other nature boy. He looked the part of the pompous American. He had this thick blond hair that he loved to comb.

Buddy always had a comb with him, and it was usually stuck in his hair, with Buddy looking in a mirror making sure his hair looked pretty. He combed his hair all the time. And I mean *all* the time. We'd be at restaurants: Buddy was combing his hair. In airports: Buddy had the comb in hand.

One night, Buddy was driving out of the arena, and he was looking in his mirror, combing his hair. He smashed into "Hacksaw" Butch Reed's personal car. Butch was once part of a great tag team, Doom, with my APA tag team partner Ron Simmons. Now it's important to understand that Butch is a very tough person. Butch wasn't exactly known for his patience. Butch beat Buddy up. In fact Butch beat up Buddy several times after this. I don't think Butch liked Buddy's hair, or maybe he was just mad at Buddy.

Either way, we invited Buddy out to eat with us with some of our mafia sponsors in Chiba, Japan, and since Butch was in the United States, Buddy agreed.

At the place we were eating, I shook hands with a man with only a thumb. In Japan, the Japanese mafia, or Yakuza, take off one of their fingers at the first knuckle and present it to the boss as a sign of loyalty. Additional fingers are taken off when a person has made a mistake, and this is their punishment.

After I shook this guy's hand, Buddy did too.

"I just shook that man's wrist," Buddy said in his megaphone-like voice.

Now I had shaken the man's wrist also, but I didn't feel the need to proclaim it out loud.

After a few glasses of sake, I asked the boss (we can all understand why I don't mention his name—I may go back to Japan one of these days) why this man was incapable of grabbing a tree limb.

"Ah," he said in soft, broken English while nodding his head and smiling, "we have many problems with that one." I guess so.

If there was ever a guy that needed to change his ways to get a different result, it was the fingerless man. Who knows what they were going to cut off next? Fingerless Mafia Man had gotten to that point because of certain choices.

Once you realize that you have to start doing things different, if you want different results, then you need to understand the difference between hard work and smart hard work. Those changes have to involve smart hard work. Don't confuse that with hard work. It's not the same thing. Let's say you're building a house in Texas. Do you just start stacking piles of bricks in the Texas summer? That is certainly hard work. Or do you make a blueprint and know exactly where on the foundation you're supposed to put those bricks? You're going to have to stack the bricks anyway. You might as well just do it once and put them where they're supposed to go. It's hard work either way, but doing it with the blueprint is the much smarter way.

Growing up in Sweetwater, it seemed like I always had a job. It started when I was ten. Child labor law enforcers would go nuts about this nowadays, but this was West Texas, and those were different times. I worked at a local golf course washing golf carts, recharging cart batteries—whatever the pro asked me to do.

The one chore everyone hated was picking up range balls. If you had to pick up range balls, it was like you had drawn the shortest straw. I got my share of time in on the range, and it wasn't much fun. What was enjoyable was when I found out that if you picked up range balls, you got your regular pay plus an extra quarter for every bucket you picked up. After I found that out, I started volunteering to pick up range balls. I quickly tripled my salary and made a lot more than the older guys. I was still working hard, but now I was also working smart and getting paid a lot more for my efforts.

Picking up range balls wasn't a lot of fun, but it taught me a lesson about being smart about your work. It also taught me to keep my pay secret.

Maybe I'm the only one who hears all the complaining that goes on. I hear people griping about how much money they make or where they work. Yet they won't make a change, and still they expect things to miraculously change.

Dr. Jung is right—everyone has problems; it is how you deal with those problems that makes your situation good or bad.

When I was in college at Abilene, I got one of the greatest pieces of advice and saw how it is applied. That year we started recruiting boys that looked good in khakis rather than in shoulder pads. I could tell that my offensive line coach, Bob Shipley, was having a hard time dealing with the direction of the program.

Bob had become one of my best friends there at Abilene, and

"Battleship" Bob Shipley and the ACU offensive line, with me. I'm second on the right.

later was a groomsman in my wedding. He was a standout football player and shot putter at ACU when I was a kid. I remember going to games and hearing fans yelling, "Give it to the Battleship." I liked him then and came to really respect him when I played for him.

One day he pulled me aside and told me he wasn't happy with his job situation. While he didn't like the hand he was dealt, he said, his only options were either to quit or to come to work and do his best. He told me that when things got tough, you don't gripe about them. You analyze your situation and choose your best option.

Griping doesn't help your situation, and it certainly isn't going to make your workplace any more enjoyable. It just seems, for some reason, that people enjoy griping. That's the easy way out. It's much easier to point out what's wrong rather than to suggest and initiate change. It's amazing to me that people expect things to get better, yet they continue doing the same things. You have to know exactly where you are now, so that you can plan your future. The financial future that will be free of worry starts with your present condition, and this involves your workplace. It's hard not to gripe sometimes about where you are, but it won't help your situation.

Bad Days at WWE

A few years ago a guy named Vince Russo somehow worked his way to the top of WWE creative writing team. Now Russo didn't like Ron or me. In fact, he went as far as to say (not to me, of course—he was definitely a coward's coward) that anyone with a southern twang sounded like an imbecile. He didn't even like Jim Ross because he was from the South, and Jim is recognized as the best play-by-play guy in wrestling history.

When Russo was a big part of making the creative decisions, I only had two options, the way I looked at it: quit, or go to work, do the best I could, and hope the situation would change.

During that time, I often thought of "Battleship" Bob Shipley's advice about how griping gets you nowhere. I loved being in WWE. My problem was just with one person. I wasn't going to complain.

Now don't think I hated Russo, but if I saw him in the desert and he was dying of thirst, I would give him peanut butter. If he were drowning I would throw him a cinder block. If he were on fire, I wouldn't . . . oh well, you get the idea.

Ron has pretty simple advice for guys that complain around him.

"You like that house you're living in? You like that car you're driving?" Ron asks. "Then don't complain. Just do your job."

That was my only option. I didn't enjoy Vince Russo, but I enjoyed my job. It did me no good to complain about it. Had I griped and not done anything about it, I would have remained in the same position. Remember, you can't get different results if you don't do anything different.

Fortunately things changed for me when Russo pulled a power play and went to our competition. He proved his genius, however; our ratings soared when he left, and the ratings of the group he went to dropped through the floor.

Ron and I threw quite a party when Vince left. I hope nothing else bad happens to him—I don't think my liver can take it.

Now, there are going to be times when bad luck falls your way. It just happens. That's when you have to roll with the punches and deal with the hand you were dealt. Remember, the past is something you can't control, you only have control over the future.

You Mean the Indians Gave Us Food and Then We Killed Them?

In 1995 I was working for Otto Wanz and Peter William in Europe when I realized that it was Thanksgiving Day back home. I was talking with Dave "Fit" Finlay, who now works with WWE— one of the all-time greats in the wrestling business, and a real good guy as well. When I told Dave, "Happy Thanksgiving," Dave asked me how come Thanksgiving was so special to us. He wanted to know why it was such a moment of celebration for Americans.

"We celebrate because around this time, the settlers that came over from England were about to spend their first winter in the colonies, and they were about to starve," I told him. "The Indians came along and in a great act of grace gave the settlers food to last through the winter." I went on to explain that we've celebrated every year to give thanks for how kind the Indians were to our ancestors. "Hence the name Thanksgiving."

"That's a neat story," Dave said. "What happened next?"

"We took all their food, shot the Indians, and took their land."

"No, no, what really happened?"

"That's what happened."

"That's not a very good holiday."

Guess Dave had a point. The Indians had no control over what happened. Of course, I really don't understand the whole situation. The Indians had the women do all the work while the men hunted all day. Does it really get any better than that? That sounds like the ultimate beer commercial to me.

I don't mean to make light of what happened to the Native Americans. It was certainly wrong, but things are going to happen to you that are wrong. I know that this is a bad illustration, but it was the only place I could fit this story into the book.

You have to plan for things to happen in your future that may not be ideal. You can't price perfection into any part of your future. When I was playing professional football, I priced perfection into my future: I assumed that everything would always go like it had always gone. I made a mistake. Anytime you price perfection into your future, it generally ends up being a mistake.

There is almost always going to be some sort of setback. Expect it, but plan for it and be versatile enough that you are able to make adjustments. If you don't have a contingency plan, then any setback will catch you unaware and unprepared.

This is where you can learn from the past but not dwell on it. I am sure that, as with everyone, things have happened to you that were not what you wanted. It is inevitable that at some point things will happen to you again that you don't expect. You should prepare for those things now. I am certainly not advocating being paranoid, just prepared.

Preparation means you don't lose sleep over the future. Being paranoid means you lose sleep because of the future.

Having your finances in order allows you to weather the storm when bad things happen to you.

Jerry Lawler's Bad Day

While you cannot expect to get different results from doing the same thing, change without a plan is not a good thing either. Financial and career success is achieved without impulse decisions.

One of the worst cases of bad luck on an impulse decision happened to Jerry Lawler one day at one of our television tapings. Jerry is one of the best color commentators there has ever been, and he and Jim Ross made a great team for our television show. Blessed with a great mind and a quick wit that few people possess, Jerry probably could have had his job forever. The problem arose when it turned out that WWE was going to let Jerry's wife go; as it appeared to me, at least, she had become too hard to deal with, and they had decided to fire her. From my perspective this seemed justified.

Jerry, staying by his wife's side, told Vince McMahon that he would have to let him go as well. Now Vince, in my opinion, is a great guy to work for; he has gone to great lengths to take care of those guys who work for him. However, he is not a guy to back into a corner. Vince is not a person who lacks testicular fortitude, as my friend Mick Foley might say.

According to Jerry's own account, Vince said he was sorry, but he would be forced to honor his request. Jerry stated that he would be on our competition's show the next Monday. In Jerry's mind he was doing the right thing by standing by his wife.

Unfortunately for Jerry, Vince was in negotiations to buy our competition, unbeknownst to Jerry. Within a month Vince had indeed bought the competition, and now Jerry had cut off the only bridge in town. About a month later, Jerry's wife left him.

I felt sorry for Jerry; I certainly wished him the best. I am sure he didn't want to be in this book as an example of what can happen when you make impulse decisions.

Fortunately, this story has a very happy ending. Jerry took a few months off and then came back to work for WWE. Now he and Jim Ross are once again the greatest commentating team in wrestling history.

Kerry Von Erich once told me that he wanted to be reincarnated as a carpenter so that he could rebuild all the bridges that he had burned.

What happened to Jerry has happened to many people, but not all these stories end up as pleasant as Jerry's did. Bad things happen to good people sometimes.

Later on, I will show you how to prepare for financial disaster. There is no one sure way to prepare for it. The only certain part about it is that you have to have some sort of plan. You can't price perfection into your future.

The main thing to realize is that where you are is where you are. There is nothing you can do about the past; you can only influence the future. You must play the hand dealt to you to your advantage. It will take a little introspection to know exactly where you stand now. Remember, it isn't where you are that is important; it is where you are headed.

Summary

- **The past cannot be changed, you can only look forward to the future, which you *can* influence.**

- **If you always do what you have always done, you will always get what you have always gotten.**

- **You have to know where you are now, so that you can chart a course as to where you want to go.**

- **Don't price perfection into your future.**

- **Don't back Vince into a corner.**

- **If you want a successful wrestling business, make sure your competition hires Vince Russo.**

- **Don't work for Iceman King Parsons.**

- **If you are outnumbered in a bar fight, make sure Ron Simmons is on your side.**

CHAPTER | 2

WHO MURDERED THE BULL?

The Visiting Team Always Gets
the Worst Dressing Rooms

I was sitting in a tiny dressing room in the Plaza del Toros, the famous bullfighting ring in Monterrey, Mexico, in the spring of 1993. I was the Mexican heavyweight wrestling champion and had traveled to Monterrey to defend my championship against the local Mexican hero.

I didn't mind the small Plaza dressing room as much as I minded all the blood everywhere. The whole floor was covered in dried blood. The good thing was that the dressing room was small, so the floor wasn't that big. The bad thing was, the floor was still covered in blood.

There had been a bullfight at the Plaza earlier that day, or perhaps the day before—I am not good at forensics, so I really didn't know how old the blood was. I only was hoping that the blood belonged to the bull, not the matador. Either way, I was somehow stuck in the dressing room in which they had butchered the bull.

I was in Mexico wrestling because the wrestling business had taken a downturn in Texas, and it was tough to make a living. At three dollars a night, wrestling was going to have to improve a whole bunch. I don't consider myself high-maintenance, but I at least like to eat.

I knew that Mexico, like Japan, was a wonderful opportunity to learn a great deal. I knew that I was going to have to learn a great deal more ("paying my dues," they always say—which translates as "starving") to reach my ultimate goal of making it to WWE. However, my main priority was not to learn, but more simply to pay my rent and eat.

I knew that the learning process didn't always involve a lot of comfort. I was just surprised at how little comfort I actually had that particular night in Mexico. I felt like I was going to be visited by the International Red Cross at any moment. If I had been a prisoner of war, the Geneva Convention definitely would have been violated.

I was thinking this situation was pretty bad. But it got worse. The local promoter came to inform me that when I entered the ring that night, the strobe lights would not be used. Instead, all the house lights would be turned on when I made my entrance. When I questioned the promoter, he told me that he felt that if the lights were to go dark during my entrance, even for a moment, I probably would be stabbed.

The promoter thought this would be bad for business. I thought it would be bad, too. Not for business, but for me.

That night things got worse, as they usually did when I was in Mexico. I got hit over the head with a metal chair and was bleeding pretty badly. Luckily, the blood was hard to notice on the dressing room floor because it was already covered with blood.

Several of the arenas in the United States allow the doctor to sew up guys on site. To what I thought was my good fortune, the arena in Mexico was the same way. I *thought* this was good fortune—until I saw the doctor. His apron was completely saturated with blood. I think I had discovered who had butchered the bull. (I was still taking for granted that it was not the matador.) Or perhaps the doctor had just returned from a MASH war unit.

I quickly decided that I really didn't need stitches that badly. In fact, I decided that I probably could wait until I got back to Texas to see a medical doctor that didn't also work on farm animals. I also concluded that my days as a *luchador* (Mexican wrestler) were just about over.

I had plenty of time that night to think about retiring from my stint in Mexico. As usual, once the match was over, I had to wait several hours for the fans waiting for me outside my dressing room to leave. By the time the last match ended, the people were usually pretty drunk, and they hadn't had quite enough. So they would sit outside my dressing room and wait on me. Not for autographs—I was a *rudo* (bad guy), not a *technico* (good guy)—but to throw things at me. You see, the Mexican people are very proud people, and I was there to beat up their local hero. I was your typical Texas gringo bad guy. The people there really did not like me, which showed I was doing my job.

However, I was really beginning not to like them either, which showed nothing except for the fact that I didn't like them. I knew sooner or later that their beer would run out or they would get bored and go home.

Mexico and Texas have a long history of not getting along. Many wars have been fought between the two. Of course, Texas has won all of them.

I also had time to think that it was a good thing the maid hadn't come yet to clean up the bull blood. That way, all the blood coming out of my head onto the floor wasn't as noticeable.

I did learn several things in Mexico, though. If I beat the local hero, most of the fans, who were very drunk, would wait for me till the wee hours of the morning outside of my dressing room to throw things at me. However, if I lost, not only was it much safer, but I also got to bed earlier.

Either way, win or lose, I really did not want to be there.

You Mean They Take Bribes?

I also learned that when the brownshirts, as custom officials were dubbed, came in and asked me for my work papers (the same work papers that the local boss claimed he had for me), I should play very dumb and tell them that I spoke no Spanish. They would then go to my boss, and he would pay them some money so they would leave. It didn't take me long to come to the conclusion that I didn't have work papers.

Finally, I learned how the promoters in Mexico kept American wrestlers from going to the competition. If a wrestler tried to leave to go to another wrestling promotion, then the boss would call the local brownshirts and tell them that he had no work papers. The wrestler would be deported.

I am sure that this was the first time that the local custom officials had any knowledge of this illegal event.

It was an amazing thing to watch these promoters somehow lose the ability to speak English when you wanted to talk to them about either money or work papers promised to you. Their English would be very good when they wanted to tell you something, but somehow it would get so broken that it was almost incomprehensible when you wanted something from them. I am sure their linguistic difficulties were purely coincidental.

Now, don't get me wrong. I'm not saying that the wrestling promoters that I worked for in Mexico (and I did just work for a relative few) were crooked. What I *am* saying is that they would have to be more honest to be crooks. They were way past crooked. They made Al Capone look like the pope.

Even at the very best, Mexico was not a good place to be for a guy portraying a bad guy beating up the local Mexican heroes nightly. I also found out that being the Mexican heavyweight champion didn't pay any more than *not* being champ. It just made your bag heavier to carry, with that oversized belt.

In fact, one of the worst things about being champion was that it made the fans hate you even more. In Matamoros the fans were actually put behind chicken wire so that they couldn't throw things at the bad guys. I appreciated this, because I was definitely a bad guy. The fans there, like everywhere else, hated the bad guys. I was beginning to hate them quite a bit as well.

I didn't even win the championship in the ring. I just showed up, and the promoters handed me a championship belt. They claimed to the media that I had won the belt in Puerto Rico, which would have been hard to do, since I had never been to Puerto Rico at that time.

I won the Korean championship the same way, then lost it every night for about two weeks all over the Korean peninsula. I lost the Korean championship about ten times.

I never did win it.

Every night I would be announced as the Korean champion. The local promoter, Lee Won Pyong, who also wrestled, would beat me for the belt and become the new Korean champion. Then we would travel to the next town and repeat the process. I actually, for a change, enjoyed dealing with Mr. Pyong; he was a gracious host, and the best and most popular Korean wrestler.

Of course, dealing with Korean fans was a little easier than their Mexican counterparts. They were a little more decisive about what they wanted. After a match got a little out of hand (to say the least) in Osu, South Korea, the fans decided to join me in the dressing room by coming through the door. Fortunately, I was able to barricade the door and plan my escape through a window.

Not surprisingly, things got worse there as well. North Korea dropped out of the nonproliferation treaty that week, and South Korea mobilized their army in case of war. My biggest worry (besides being killed in a war I had no part of) was that I did not look Korean. If there ever was a perfect hostage to be on CNN held by an extremist group, I was it.

With Kerry Von Erich and Bobby Duncum Jr. at the Sportatorium. This was the day Bobby and I won our first championship belts in 1992.

Bobby Duncum Jr. and I were the only Americans I could see in South Korea, at least where we were. I might have been worrying needlessly, but two six-and-a-half-foot-tall blond-haired guys wearing cowboy hats just seemed to stick out a little too much if a war erupted between two Korean countries.

I knew where I wanted to be, and I knew that being in places like Mexico and Korea (Korea wasn't bad—I liked Korea, it was just a long way from home) was necessary to get to where I wanted to be. I understood that making it to World Wrestling Federation demanded years of a learning process, and that the learning process didn't always involve a lot of comfort or money.

I had set my goal as to where I wanted to be, and I had decided what it was worth to attain it. It would have been easier to just go to work during those days somewhere around my hometown, but then I certainly would not have had any chance of doing what I truly wanted to do.

I knew the road to success in wrestling would involve some discomfort. I knew that nothing worthwhile could be achieved easily.

However, I had no idea it would involve this much discomfort and this little money. It is amazing how easily discomfort can be tolerated when you are paid well. It wasn't that I hated what I was doing—I was headed in the right direction careerwise, and I actually enjoyed these times—it was just a bit unnerving wondering if you were going to get stabbed that night, or if the wrong brownshirt would show up and take you to jail, or a war would break out and you would end up being a hostage held by a bunch of angry Communist Koreans.

However, I also knew that if I couldn't be successful at this level, then there was no way I could be successful at the level of WWE. This, to me, was an important gauge as to how I was progressing in the wrestling business. I knew exactly where I wanted to be and for whom I wanted to work. I also knew that there were no shortcuts to get there. I had to decide if these sacrifices were worth it.

I decided that they were.

You have to be able to define what you want in life. You also have to be able to decide what it is worth to you to accomplish your goal, and what you are willing to give up now so that you can do what you would like to do in the future.

I knew being in Mexico and going through some things that weren't what I would consider ideal was necessary to get to where I wanted to be later in life. I believe that the people with all of the letters after their names call this "delayed gratification." Delayed gratification is simply doing something now that you may not like so that your future will be brighter. This future will not happen if you don't put certain things off and do what you have to do to prepare for it.

There are times in everyone's lives when they will do things that they would prefer not to do, such as going back to school at night to finish their degrees. What I was doing in Mexico was basically my schooling for a later career in WWE. Like most people going to school, I did not enjoy every minute of it. But I knew it was necessary.

Set Your Goals Before You Start

The key to looking at life is to ask yourself where you want to be five or ten years from now. That can involve some changes in what you are doing, but otherwise you will not reach the goals you have set.

The key to setting goals is to work backward.
Start with your goal. Whether it is paying off your house, paying off your credit card debt, or retiring early, start with the end result first. After you have identified your goal, plan a course to get there within a certain time limit. Perhaps you cannot pay off your debt in five years; maybe it will take ten. Figure out how long it will take so that you can make your plan.

Without a goal, you are plotting a course to nowhere.

You can decide to save more money or start paying off your debt, but without a systematic approach, you are going to be just spinning your wheels. You have to know exactly what you want so that you can make weekly or monthly spending plans to reach your goals.

It is admirable to decide to start saving money for a better future, but you need to decide what that future is. Then decide how much money you will need to achieve that future. You cannot start at square one and head off into the sunset without a plan. You must plan the destination first, then figure out how to get there. In 1992 I had only $27 in my pocket. I had gotten that way by making bad decisions. If I had kept making the same bad decisions, I would have stayed broke. I knew that I had to do something different to get different results.

Let me ask you a question.

Are you where you should or could be, at least financially, in life? If not, why not? If where you are is not where you could be, then you have to decide to change something. You can't get different results from doing the same things. The definition of insanity is expecting different results from doing the same things.

Where would you like to be ten years from now?

Now ask yourself, what is the best route to get there? You have to decide what it is worth to reach your goals, and what you are willing to put off buying or spending to make these goals a reality.

Remember, though, be sensible.

For example, if you make $5,000 a month and you want to save more money, don't blindly decide one day to start saving $4,000 out of each check. You are setting yourself up for failure. Make a sensible long-term plan. You will have to alter your lifestyle to do this. The key is to alter your lifestyle to the point that you can still enjoy living your life. Determine on a piece of paper what it is worth to you to reach your goals and what is a reasonable way to achieve your goals.

Nobody gets to his or her goals by accident. You must first decide where you want to be, and then plot out your route to get there.

Sir Edmund Hillary didn't just decide one day to climb Mount Everest. It took years of planning. You must have a plan. This plan will always involve a little delayed gratification. Believe me, if the end result is worth it to you, then you won't mind what you have to go through to achieve your goal.

Nice Hit, Now Please Hit the Other Team

You also must define what is important. In spring camp with the Los Angeles Raiders, I made a mistake one day and went the wrong direction. As big as the playbook was, I thought I was doing good just lining up in the right spot.

It is important to understand that I had come from a small Division II school, and being with the team of my dreams was a bit overwhelming. Lining up and trying to compete against guys I really wanted to ask for an autograph was something to behold. Then they gave me a playbook that was bigger than the Bible. In fact, it might as well have been written in koine Greek. I was the only rookie offensive lineman in camp that year, which made me stick out even further.

Anyway, this particular day I went the wrong direction and ran over Max Montoya, who had just been acquired for a large sum of money from the Cincinnati Bengals. Kim Helton, the offensive line coach, asked me what was wrong. I told him I was confused. Helton explained to me that they had paid Max a lot of money to come to Los Angeles, and if I didn't mind, the next time I got confused, could I please do so around one of the lower-paid players? I understood at that point that you must realize *what* or *who* is important.

If I had known that Kim was the one who would later cut me, I would have run over him.

I don't believe in crash-dieting or crash-budgeting. You have to find a medium in which you can be happy as well as planning for a better, more worry-free future. Remember, if you are not where you should be financially, you will not get to where you want to be overnight. It is the same as a person who suddenly realizes they have gotten overweight. Nobody gets overweight overnight. If you didn't get that way overnight, you won't correct the problem overnight either.

I don't believe in the austerity preached in certain financial books. I believe that a future that is forty years down the road is not worth making yourself miserable over now. What happens if you never see that future? I believe you can make your world better now and assure yourself of a secure future without having to drive a twenty-year-old car and live in a shack.

I do drive a twenty-year-old truck, but I have had it for twenty years. I drove the same truck to Los Angeles, when I went to play with the Raiders. I just can't seem to let it go. I was visiting John Buesing, my old college roommate, one year and he asked me what I had done with "that old truck I used to drive." I told him

I had driven it up to see him. John laughed and called me a bunch of names. I want to make this clear: he was laughing *at* me, not *with* me. I still have the truck because of nostalgic reasons, not because I am cheap. In fact, I plan to give that truck to John in my will, and I hope the gas tank is empty when he gets it. I also hopes it breaks down.

I believe that you have to enjoy life now, because if you are not enjoying yourself now, you will not enjoy life later when you achieve the goals that you have set for yourself. A person needs to take every opportunity to enjoy his current world. There is no guarantee you will be here in the future.

Robert Burns once wrote, "I would rather be a bright comet burning across the sky bright for everyone to see, than a dead void planet that lives forever in darkness."

I believe you have to live, not just exist.

That being said, I don't believe there is an excuse to be negligent in planning for your future. I just believe that you can't make yourself miserable planning for your retirement; there is a happy medium. Many books teach you to be "retirement poor," saving so much of your income that there is nothing left with which to enjoy life now. I believe this contradicts what life is all about.

The problem with sacrificing too much now is that you develop the habit of always sacrificing and being unhappy. When you retire you will still be unhappy, because that is how you have preconditioned yourself to be.

If you find a medium *now* so you can be happy and prepare for your future, then you will find that this will continue throughout your life. Remember, I am not talking about a quick fix, but rather an altered lifestyle with which you can live.

You have to decide what is important to you now and how that fits into your future. Sometimes preparing for your future takes a little sacrifice. While each person is different, you will have to decide for yourself what you are willing to do to prepare financially for your future.

While you are deciding what it is worth to you to make your future better, remember that you still have to live now.

I have always loved to travel. I enjoy seeing different cultures and being part of different communities. I have enjoyed the trips I have been fortunate enough to make to Wales, where I had the opportunity to go to a local pub and play snooker with some Welsh gentlemen. I enjoyed the trip to the wine country of Styria in southern Austria with Otto Wanz and the trip to visit the U.S. troops in Afghanistan at Christmastime. I would rather immerse myself in a culture than attend some fancy bar or party where the local culture is piped in just for the tourists.

Travel should be a learning experience, just like life, that makes your life better. It all ties in with the questions: Are you just going to watch life, or are you going to experience it? Are you going to sit on the fence, or will you ride? Those that choose to ride sometimes fall off, but at least they don't get splinters. Believe me, no one will show up to watch people sit on a fence. They *will* show up to watch someone ride.

Travel to me is not worth much if you choose to ignore the local customs and local religions and just eat in American restaurants. Travel, like life, is not a destination but an experience. You have to enjoy the ride.

A number of years ago WWE was doing a tour in South Africa. I planned on staying a few extra days and going to see Victoria Falls, so I flew my parents and my wife down to see me at the end of the tour. My father has been many places in his life, but he has generally hated going to every one of them. He loves it once he gets there, but all of the problems with travel make him just want to stay home. He is very nervous about problems arising. Because of this, he is the type of traveler that gets to the airport several hours early. I am not this type of traveler.

We had stayed in Benoni, just outside of Johannesburg, for a couple of days with some friends, Al and Donna Horne. Al and Donna went to college with my parents at Abilene Christian University. Al then returned, with Donna, to be a missionary in South Africa. Al trains the local people through a four-year college curriculum to go back to their homes and build churches. If some of these televangelists typify everything that is wrong with religion, then Al would typify everything that is right. Heaven is reserved for people like Al.

At Victoria Falls with my dad, on the border of Zambia and Botswana.

We also got to spend time with Dr. and Mrs. Lawrence Van Druten, the parents of Richard Van Druten, one of my best friends from college. I don't believe Dr. Van Druten butchered bulls.

Our trip had been just perfect. We had just returned from Victoria Falls (the waterfalls that border Zimbabwe and Zambia—three times as high as Niagara Falls and more than a mile wide) and were to fly out the next day. Our flight was later in the day, so I figured we had plenty of time to go and visit Sun City, a fabulous resort just outside of Johannesburg. Al arranged for us to borrow a van from one of his church people. Needless to say, my father was not thrilled with this. His plans were to spend the day at the airport, waiting for the flight.

It looked as if we were going to make it back to the airport in plenty of time, when the van Al had borrowed broke down in front of a squatter's camp that was notorious for crime. These squatters' camps were made up of people that had emigrated from other countries, most of them illegally, and crime was very high around them.

A large crowd was beginning to gather across the road when someone passing by recognized me. We had just done a televised special for the continent of Africa. He informed us that this was not a safe place to be. This was not news to me. He agreed to take the women and my father to get a tow truck. Al and I agreed to stay there and be robbed. I gave all of my money and my identification to my wife and said good-bye—I hoped for just a few minutes.

I told Al that adversity makes you bond with people, but that I really had no desire to bond with him that day. Fortunately, our group found a tow truck very quickly, and by the time they had returned there was a very big crowd waiting to rob us.

The guy who stopped took us straight to the airport, and we just barely made our flight. I told my dad, "See, we had plenty of time to go to Sun City."

Dad has not traveled with me since.

While I don't agree with going out of your way to put yourself in dangerous places, neither should you risk your retirement by not saving now because you are spending everything you make. I do believe you should experience everything you possibly can. You have to make the most out of everything, and that includes when you are doing things that you would prefer not to do so you may secure your future.

There are certain things you will do now that you would prefer not to do, because you know the direction you are headed. The road getting to where you want to be should be enjoyable; sometimes as much enjoyment will be achieved by getting there as by being there. I have seen too many people die while waiting for retirement to know that you must be happy now. Believe me, if you are not happy now, you will not be happy in different circumstances. It is important not to make yourself miserable in the process of saving for your future.

Of course, if you are going to be happy anyway, you might as well be rich and happy. Read on—we are getting there.

Summary

- Set your goals and then work backward to find the best way to reach them.

- Delayed gratification can be a useful thing to remember when planning for your future.

- The definition of insanity is expecting different results from the same actions.

- Nobody gets to his or her goals by mistake.

- If you are not happy now, you will not be happy later.

- Don't beat the local Mexican hero in his hometown.

- There's always enough time to go to Sun City.

CHAPTER 3

THE WATER IS NOT THE PROBLEM

You Can Have When You Have

If your boat springs a leak, bailing out water is only a temporary solution. To have a dry, seaworthy boat, you must first plug the leak. Only then will bailing out water do any long-term good. There are many very good and proven ways to get water out of a boat. Most of these methods certainly will work—if, and only if, the boat does not still have a hole in it.

Likewise, there are many very good and proven ways to reduce debt if, and only if, your financial boat is seaworthy.

Neither the most efficient bilge pump nor the fastest person bailing water will be able to keep all of the water out of the boat until the leak has been fixed. While you may not sink if you bail water continuously, you quickly will realize that you are not working very intelligently, *and* you are getting very tired. In fact, it seems ridiculous to even think about bailing water until you plug the leak. However, this is exactly what people who are in debt do. They bail and bail, but it is futile work because the leak has not been plugged.

The water in the boat is a result of the problem, not the problem itself. This is an easy mistake to make: the water definitely *looks* like the problem. As my friend Mutt used to say, "You have to look past the door." It is very easy to see all that water and think the water is your problem. Once you try to bail it out and the boat fills back up, you realize that you have a much bigger problem.

If you bail the water out, you have solved nothing. You have only postponed the inevitable: *the boat will continue taking on water.*

Aspirin for Your Tumor?

If a person with a brain tumor is suffering from a headache, for temporary relief, you may give this person an aspirin. Long-term, though, the aspirin will not help. It may help the headache immediately, but this is misleading. When the headache comes back, you believe this person needs another aspirin. Soon, though, you realize that the headaches just keep coming back no matter how much aspirin is administered. You must go to the root of the problem, the tumor.

People who have gotten themselves into debt often mistakenly believe that the whole problem is their debt. This is incorrect. Debt is merely the first thing you notice, just like the first thing you notice is the headache or the water in the boat. The debt is a symptom of the problem, not the problem itself.

Bobby's Evil Echo

Several years ago my good friend Bobby Duncum Jr. was in Japan, calling home to visit with his wife. The thing Bobby didn't realize was that there was a delay on the phone that he was using, which caused an echo.

This caused quite a problem because before Bobby's wife, Michelle, could answer, Bobby heard himself on the phone. It went something like this:

"Hello?" And the echo, "Hello?"

Bobby responded, "Who is this?" And the echo, "Who is this?"

Bobby then said, agitatedly, "This is Bob." And the echo said, "This is Bob."

Bobby then hung up the phone after a few more choice words. When Bobby got down to the bus to go to the next town, several of his buddies asked Bobby what was wrong. He replied, "It wasn't enough that she had someone in my house, but he was mimicking me." Bobby later got it figured out and has been much happier since.

Bobby needed to look past the echo.

When your financial boat is sinking, it is hard to look past the water to see that the problem is the hole in the bottom of the

Booker T, Buddy Landell, James Beard, Bobby Duncum Jr., and me in front of the largest Shinto shrine in Tokyo, 1993.

boat. You must look past your boatload of debt to see that the problem is the incurrence of debt, not the debt itself. Dealing with the debt itself is a quick fix that won't last. You must deal with the cause, not the effect.

It is easy to be overcome with the predicament of your overwhelming debt and never see that your whole problem is the incurrence of debt. When you are standing in a boat full of water, it is easy to assume that you will be safe if you just bail the water out of the boat. It is important to understand the difference between the symptom and the problem.

The key to being out of debt is first to stop incurring debt. Being free of debt involves dealing with the financial tumor and then worrying about the financial headache. The key is to quit causing debt to accumulate. Then you can work on eliminating your debt forever.

It sounds simple, except for the fact that recognizing the problem and determining to break old habits, while simple in theory, is not always easy in reality.

Living Within Your Means

The whole key is to quit spending the money you don't have. When you have the material means to pay for something you want, *then* you can have it. *You can have when you have.* Otherwise, you are just springing another leak.

I said this was simple, but remember, I didn't say it was painless. It sounds very easy to just wait until you have the money to buy something, but in America today it is one of the hardest things to accomplish. When you have the means to buy something, you can buy it. In other words, when you *have* you may *have.*

This simply involves living within your means. Do not spend more than you make. If you make $100,000 a year, the key to not creating more debt is to live on less than $100,000. If you make $20,000 a year, live on less than $20,000. Sound simple? Then why are so many people in debt?

People that are making $50,000 believe that if they were just making $100,000 a year, then their problems would be solved. This usually does not work. Habits of spending more than you make at a lower salary typically stay with you when you are earning more. The salary is not the problem. The problem is spending more than you bring home.

Often, it does not benefit those with credit card problems to have someone pay off their debts. This just allows them to charge more. To help these people, first teach them to live within their means. Then, and only then, will paying off their debt be of any long-term help.

Paying off debt will provide temporary relief, but it *will* be temporary. You are treating the symptom, not the problem. If you have a problem with incurring debt, the only way to get out of the problem is to first quit incurring debt. Only then will you be able to treat symptoms like credit problems and mountainous debt.

Different Size Holes in Your Boat

A lot of people have no idea how much debt they actually have. All they see is a whole ocean of water.

There are also a lot of people that just see debt as debt and do not realize that there are different types of debt. Just as there can be different types of holes that let water into the boat, some holes can be bigger than others. It is important to find out where most of the water is leaking out of the boat.

Odds are, if you are like most people, you have some credit card debt. Odds also are that this is the biggest hole in your boat.

Most people don't realize how bad credit card debt can really be. Most credit card companies offer an introductory rate that is pretty good—such as 1.9 to 3.9 percent, a very good rate. The problem is, these low rates are introductory rates, which means they don't last.

After a period of time, usually six months, this rate goes up significantly to something around 18 or 19 percent. You would get a better rate from Tony Soprano. To show you how much this actually costs you, let me show you a few things.

Let's say you have a total balance of $5,000 in credit card debt that is carried at 19 percent interest. If you decide to pay off that $5,000 debt by sending in $100 a month, it will take you more than eight years to pay it off. Plus, you will have spent right at $10,000 to pay off the original debt. No wonder there are so many credit card companies.

If you send in just $80 a month toward this $5,000 debt, it will take you almost twenty-five years to pay off this debt. Plus, you will have spent right at $24,000 to pay off the original debt.

There are people who are paying this tiny amount, percentage wise, toward their credit card debt without ever realizing how much they actually have to pay to get rid of their debt.

It gets much worse the more you owe. If you owe $10,000 and you can only afford to pay $200 per month toward your debt, it will take you more than eight years to pay off that debt. Now, if this is all that you can afford to pay, then by all means pay what you can; however, understand you will end up paying over $19,000 to retire that $10,000 debt.

Can you understand why it is so important for your financial security to pay off your high-interest debt? If you don't stop incurring this debt, then you have a huge hole in your boat that is next to impossible to plug.

The credit card companies love people who pay the minimum amount toward their bill each month. They make a lot of money off these people. The bottom line is, it is important to get rid of all your high-interest debt first. Pay enough each month to get rid of it in a timely fashion.

There are many ways to lower your interest rate. One is to transfer your balance to a lower-interest-rate card. However, understand that most likely the lower interest on this card has a fixed time limit. If you cannot pay off your debt in the allotted time, then you might want to transfer the amount again to another card, if possible.

There is also a home equity loan. A home equity loan is one of the better loans available, as you will get a much lower interest rate than you would on your credit cards, and it is tax-deductible.

I would be hesitant about doing this, however, because the collateral you are putting up is your home. If you default on a home equity loan, you could lose your home. I just don't believe it is a wise thing to put your home at risk because of your debt. Being in debt is the result of bad decisions; making another potentially bad decision is not the key to getting out of debt.

There is an amortization chart (see page 80) that will show you what you have to pay each month with certain interest being charged to pay off your debt in a timely fashion. To figure out what you will pay in total, simply add all the payments together.

For example, if you have to pay $100 a month to get rid of a certain debt in five years, then multiply 12 months times $100, which equals $1,200. Then multiply that figure by the year period ($1,200 × 5 years = $6,000).

One thing that a lot of people don't realize is that interest accrues daily. If you get paid twice a month or once a week, then it is prudent to send money in weekly or biweekly according to what you can afford. In this way you limit, to a degree, the effect of compounding interest.

Many people believe that things will get better for them all of a sudden. Many believe that their ships are bound to come in someday and erase all of their financial worries. If you are one of

AMORTIZATION CHART

6%	1 Year	5 Years	10 Years	20 Years
1,000	86.07	19.34	11.11	7.17
2,000	172.13	38.64	22.21	14.33
5,000	430.33	96.67	55.52	35.83
10,000	860.66	193.33	111.03	71.65
20,000	721.33	386.66	222.05	143.29

12%	1 Year	5 Years	10 Years	20 Years
1,000	88.83	22.25	14.35	11.02
2,000	117.70	44.49	28.70	22.03
5,000	444.24	111.23	71.74	55.06
10,000	888.49	222.45	143.48	110.11
20,000	1776.98	444.89	286.95	220.22

18%	1 Year	5 Years	10 Years	20 Years
1,000	91.68	25.40	18.02	15.44
2,000	183.36	50.79	36.04	30.87
5,000	458.40	126.97	90.10	77.17
10,000	916.80	253.94	180.19	154.34
20,000	1833.60	507.87	360.38	308.67

these people, then let me ask you, How have things changed for you in the past? If your circumstances have not changed significantly, then they probably won't change in the future, either. You will have to initiate your own change to improve your life.

That is why I am writing this book.

Those that are always waiting on some fortune to come in will never help themselves. If you currently are not doing the correct things with your money, then if you have more money, you will just be able to screw up on an even bigger scale. This can be fun, except when you realize that you have blown an opportunity to make your life better.

You have to learn to live within your means. This means you will not be buying things you cannot afford. Otherwise, the only certainty in life is that you will never be debt-free or financially independent.

Some debt will be necessary in your lifetime, at least, for most people. Very few people will be able to pay cash for their first house or their first car. A mortgage is something most people will have, because very few people will have the cash to pay for their home. Most people will have a car payment as well.

Certain debt is acceptable as long as you have the cash flow to maintain it. However, this is not the type of debt that is sinking most people in America today. We will discuss this type of debt in a little bit. For now, we will concentrate on the type of debt that causes problems for most people.

Many people simply do not know how much money they spend or how much extra money they actually have each month. The worksheet (see page 82) will help you determine your monthly total expenditures.

Before you can plug the leak, you must realize where the leak is. It won't do you any good if you are trying to fix a leak where the leak isn't. You must determine where your extra money is going.

Understand that it is not always easy to figure out exactly how much you spend a month, because some of your expenses fluctuate. However, you should know exactly how much you spend

MONTHLY EXPENDITURE WORKSHEET

MORTGAGE OR RENT:	$
CABLE OR SATELLITE:	$
CAR LOANS:	$
INSURANCE (car, health, home, other):	$
UTILITIES (gas, electric, water):	$
PHONE:	$
OTHER LOANS:	$
CREDIT CARD PAYMENTS:	$
OTHER PAYMENTS (layaways, boat, household appliances, etc.):	$
TOTAL:	$

*An extra copy can be found in the back of the book.

per month on certain expenses, such as a mortgage, car loans, insurance, and any other set payments. You need to know exactly how much has to be taken out of your income each month so you will know how much is left over for hard-to-estimate extras, such as dining out and clothing expenses.

Once you can figure out your monthly expenses—and that is what this chart is for—then you will be able to establish how much extra money you should have. The problem is that the extra money most people should have has a hard time materializing. So you have to ask yourself, Where did it go?

One of the worst things you can do is to carry excess cash. Now, I am a firm believer in paying cash for everything you possibly can, but this does not mean to carry enough cash with you to purchase a car. If you have cash with you, it becomes very easy to spend. Often, this type of spending is on purchasing things that you do not necessarily need. In other words, the worst type of spending: impulse spending.

Two Million Pesos, a Border Town, and a Steak Knife

There was a time when I carried a lot of cash, but not necessarily by choice. I was working in Mexico at many of the border towns like Matamoros and Nuevo Laredo, which are notorious for crime. In fact, they put the crowd behind chicken wire so they couldn't throw things at me.

I really didn't believe I could trust anyone. The government officials were crooked, the promoter was certainly crooked, and the fans had to be put behind chicken wire. Do you blame me?

This was before the peso was devalued. I got paid in cash the last night before I wrestled. I would usually get around 2,100,000 pesos, which was a large stack of money—approximately $700. The problem was, I couldn't put this money in my bag because I didn't know who would be in the dressing room while I was wrestling. So, I would take out a bunch of tape—in front of everyone, so that everyone would know there was no money in my bag—and I would tape the money to my ankles.

My boots barely fit over this huge wad of bills. When I came out of the ring, I would put the money in my bag, next to the knife I had borrowed from the local steakhouse, and leave the arena.

I understand there are times when you have to carry a lot of cash, but I also think these are the exceptions. If you are in Matamoros and get paid in pesos, this could be one of those times.

Small Things Aren't So Small over Time

My advice is to carry just enough cash for what you need today. Spending this extra cash may seem insignificant at the time, but over the course of a month, it can become quite a sum.

Think about this: If you buy just one thing a day for five dollars that you really do not need, it doesn't seem like much at first. This could be a number of things. Maybe a couple of bottled waters, a loaded cappuccino, a strawberry and banana smoothie, or even a Jack and Coke at the bar. Five dollars a day would add up to over $1,800 a year. Now it starts to become expensive to have that extra Jack and Coke at lunch.

I understand that this is a small thing, and it is just an illustration, but it shows how small things add up over time.

Look up how many ATM charges you had last month, and the fees that each withdrawal cost you. This is something that you have a hard time including on your monthly expenditure worksheet. However, it is an example of small things that end up being not so small. Twenty dollars here and twenty dollars there do not seem like much, but this could be where your extra cash is going. It certainly could be one of the leaks, even if it is not the main one.

You have to stop the leak, then get the water out. You have to find out where you are spending your extra money. Is it on sales each month at your favorite department store? Is it a night out each week with the boys or with friends? If you should have extra money and you don't, then you have to figure out why you don't have that extra money.

If you are paying cash for things and don't have any extra money each month, then at least you have made sure you are not incurring more debt. This is good.

You will never go into debt by buying something with cash. Whether this is a wise purchase or not is a different matter. Whether you are spending money you should be saving is a different matter, also. But at least if you are learning to "have when you have," you won't be springing a new leak. While you may not be getting ahead with your savings, you won't be getting behind either. My advice is to pay cash for things and find a way to save money also. Once you get into the habit of paying cash, then you will know that if you don't have the money to buy something, then you can't have that thing. You will realize that the money you are saving each month is money that you don't need and won't miss.

Give Yourself a Pay Cut

If your boss came in one day and told you that it was necessary to lower your salary by 5 or 10 percent, you would adjust. You would have no choice. In fact, your quality of life probably would not be diminished in the least. After a while, you would not even miss the money that you had been making.

To stop incurring debt, you need to lower your own salary and put that 5 or 10 percent toward savings or toward reducing any current debt. If you are spending more than you earn, then you certainly have to lower your expenditures enough so that you no longer live beyond your means. Just as you eventually would adapt to a lower salary forced on you by your boss, you will also become accustomed to spending less. You will be surprised how this will affect not only your current lifestyle but also your future.

We will discuss a systematic savings and debt-reduction plan in the next chapter.

Some kinds of debt are acceptable, but some kinds are no good at all. Sometimes you have to go into debt. Like I said, few people can pay cash for a house or car. There is a huge difference between good debt and bad debt.

Good debt, like a mortgage on a house, is paying for something that will *appreciate,* or increase in value, over time. When you pay for a house, unless you overpaid or the real estate market stumbles, that house will go up in price. This is debt that when paid off will leave you with something worthwhile, like a place to live. This is also debt that is tax-deductible, at least as far as the interest is concerned. Additionally, when this debt is paid off, you will have something worth the money you put into it.

Bad debt is just the opposite. Bad debt, like credit card debt, will leave you with nothing when it is paid off. Needless to say, the interest on this debt is not tax-deductible.

Just as in life, there are gray areas in debt. There are things you may not be able to buy with cash, such as a car. Buying a car would fall into the category of *necessary* debt, not *good* debt: the car will not appreciate over the course of the loan, as your home should. Fortunately, interest rates on car loans are usually acceptable, and you will have something of value when you pay off the loan.

Remember, there is no way you can rationalize credit card debt into this gray area. It is, and will always be, bad debt.

Europe at Ten Miles Per Hour

I lived in Europe for two years, wrestling on a European circuit. The second year I was there, I decided to buy my own car and trailer in which to live.

Very few people can afford to pay for their first house and a car as newlyweds, but we did. Of course, when you understand what I bought, you won't be quite as impressed.

We would wrestle in a town for about two months, then move to another town. Most of the Europeans had their own trailers in which they lived, as well as cars to drive. We usually would park these trailers in the parking lot behind the buildings where we were wrestling. We would be in these parking lots for as long as two months, so it made sense to have your own trailer, because this would be our home while we were there.

Just as a traveling circus or carnival would live on the grounds where the circus or carnival was set up, this is how we lived. In fact, a lot of modern-day wrestling originated in the era of trav-

Bremen, Germany: in front of my first home, all eighty-four square feet of it, including wheels.

eling carnivals. The trick of the traveling tough guy challenging some guy in the crowd was used frequently in the carnivals. It was amazing how the same guy appeared in the crowd to challenge the carnival tough guy in each town.

There is even a secret language of carnival workers, referred to as Carny, which many wrestlers use to talk to each other in front of people they don't know. Carny might be comparable to an upscale pig Latin, the playful secret language in which a syllable or two is added to a word.

Since all the Europeans had their own cars and trailers, I decided to buy my own as well. The car and trailer cost about $2,000 total. The trailer was fourteen feet long by six feet wide: a whopping 84 square feet.

My wife was extremely happy with our spacious accommodations. Of course, there were drawbacks to this rolling palace. There was no running water. We had to go each morning to get enough water to last us through the day. We had very handy jugs with nice carrying handles for this daily task.

Of course, I guess if we had filled up the water and sprinted back to the trailer holding the water, then technically we would have had running water.

We did have a bathroom. It was about a quarter of a mile down the road. Going to the bathroom in the middle of the night in northern Germany during December is very enjoyable when you have to walk a quarter of a mile across a solid ice parking lot. The good part about our spacious home was that you could reach from the bedroom through the kitchen to the dining room without ever moving from the bed. Normally when you get breakfast in bed, you might have a tray that you put next to the bed. This was similar to how our dining room was. You could reach the dining room table from the bed. However, you had to reach through the kitchen and past the pantry to do so, which was possible.

The main drawback to my palace was that there was very little insulation in the walls. During winter, if you rolled over and accidentally touched any wall, it was like touching a frozen pipe. This tended to awaken you. Since I am just over six and a half feet tall and the trailer was only six feet wide, I had to lie crossways in bed. I just loved those cold walls.

The floor was not exactly a sturdy thing to stand on either. I (being 300 pounds at the time) had to walk precisely down the center of the floor because it was the only part that seemed sturdy. Since the ceiling was barely over six feet high, the only place I could stand erect was beneath the skylight, which was less than a foot across.

Another drawback was our heater, which was originally a gas heater. The pilot would blow out during the night, and you would wake up able to see your breath in front of your face. Of course, the natural thing to do was to press the gas button and try to find the ignition in the dark. The problem was that during the time elapsed looking for the ignition, a lot of gas can build up. This can cause a nice little explosion and a pleasant little fireball in your face—extremely enjoyable at three o'clock in the morning.

I soon replaced the gas heater with an electric one. Then the only problem was that fuses blew quite regularly, but at least there were no fireballs. During the winter there were no mosquitoes, but during the summer, we actually had to put a bug light inside the trailer.

We didn't worry about fuses or fireballs during the summer. We had to wake up around eight every morning because the sun would make it too hot to be in the trailer. Obviously, we didn't have air conditioning at all.

To compensate for the lack of air conditioning, I parked our rolling home under one of the few trees in the campground. This allowed me to sleep about an extra half hour before it got too hot to stay inside. This was great until a lightning storm one night. Either lightning struck the tree or heavy winds blew it over—either way, the tree was gone. I felt like Jonah sitting outside Nineveh when the gourd vine that was shading him died. He wanted to go with it. I wasn't that bad, but I was close.

The good thing about no air conditioning was that I spent a lot of time in the swimming pool, which happened to be topless. I always lie out topless anyway. Cindy was not incredibly happy about me spending so much time at the pool, but I explained that it was the only way to stay cool. It is amazing how hot she got about me staying cool.

The car was a thing of beauty too. This is the only time I ever owned a foreign car; however, since I guess it was in a foreign country, then technically it wasn't a foreign car. I guess a Chevy would have been considered a foreign car.

Johnny South, a wrestler from Colwyn Bay, Wales, sold me that car. He told me how proud he was of it. I think he was more proud to see it go. "Those Americans, they'll buy anything."

Life Is about the Journey, Not the Destination

The passenger-side window did not work, and of course there was no air. So Cindy and I would argue over who would get to drive. The car actually wasn't big enough to pull the trailer. In fact, going through the Swiss and Bavarian Alps, the car's top speed was often 15 kilometers (approximately 10 miles) per hour. It often overheated. In fact, I got to visit a whole lot of rivers in Europe to borrow water for our car.

One day I even learned how to use one of those old water pumps to get water for our radiator. On this particular day, we also made a wrong turn and ended up in Italy. We were supposed to be going to Seeboden, Austria. I am not sure exactly what happened, but we ended up at the Italian border.

We really got to see Europe. Slowly.

The car lost compression and completely cratered a month before the end of the last tournament, just as the weather got really cold. So much for my foreign car.

If ignorance is bliss, then we must have been happily stupid, because this was one of the greatest times in our lives. We were getting to see Europe, although extraordinarily slowly, and for us this was a great treat. The people we lived around became fantastic friends. We traveled to almost every country in Europe, with almost no money, and loved every minute of it. We both became somewhat fluent in German, at least fluent enough to order pizza, beer, and ice cream.

I always have believed that happy, good people could have a good time in a ditch, while miserable people could hate life in a mansion.

This goes well with what I believe about the road to a destination, such as goals of financial success. I knew that I didn't want to continue to live in the conditions in which Cindy and I lived in Europe for the rest of our lives. However, I also knew that this was a great opportunity to visit many foreign countries, live with locals, and be a part of their communities. This was a necessary step to get to the point where World Wrestling Federation would employ me. It didn't mean I couldn't enjoy myself while getting there.

Believe me, if you don't enjoy the trip, you won't enjoy the destination. You will just find something else to dislike. I can help you get there. I can't help you enjoy life. That is a conscious decision on your part. Maybe Dr. Freud's couch is still there.

Miserable people are miserable no matter what the surroundings. Even if they are on the right road or even if they reach the destination, they will still be miserable. If you are miserable now, then getting out of debt will only help you financially, it won't make people like you.

Very few people can afford to buy both a car and a house when they first get married, but I did. I even paid cash for all of it. My wife didn't share in the enthusiasm of my accomplishment, although she still had me (she wasn't too sure about how great that was at that time, either). Cindy could have left me, but she didn't have money to get home. Besides, it would be too hard to split half of nothing if she were to leave.

Of course, the good thing about starting off so small with our first home was that anything bigger was considered a mansion. Our next home was an apartment in Athens, Texas. It was only 800 square feet, but in comparison, it seemed huge. We even had our own bathroom—indoors.

Our first real home is only 2,000 square feet, but in comparison to the apartment and the trailer, we are very happy. We have two bathrooms (both indoors) in this home. Luxury is relative, I guess.

Most people have to borrow money for their first home, as I did for my four-wheel rolling palace. The key is to understand your debt. You must know which kind of debt is not necessary for you, and which kind should definitely not be happening.

Don't Price Perfection into Your Future

Remember, if you owe money on something, you do not own that thing. You may *say* it is yours, but it is not. The person or company that loaned you the money is the one who owns what you think is yours. This will not change until you pay it off.

Debt, if used for useful, worthwhile, or needed purposes, is okay if your cash flow will allow you to pay off the debt in a timely fashion. The problem with incurring debt is the possibility that your cash flow could end for a period. Your debt may seem manageable now, but things can change. It is so much easier to buy things as you can afford them without going into debt. *You can have when you have.* That means when you have the cash to pay for something, then buy it—not before.

Typically, people want it all *now.* Instead of buying a home and furnishing it as they can afford it, they want it all done immediately. So they go into debt, and often foolishly.

Buying nice things for a house costs money. Too many times, we try to buy too much at once and skimp on quality. We will buy a house full of furniture that is not of the highest quality because we believe that is what we are supposed to do.

The problem with this is that ten years from now, you will be replacing this furniture, and you will be no better off. The smart thing to do is to buy things as you can afford them. *You can have when you have*—even if it is just a couch, an occasional chair, or a dining room table a year. After ten years, you will have a house full of nice furniture, debt-free. Then there will be those who see your house and they will go into helpless debt trying to imitate you. The difference is that *you* won't owe a dime.

Impulse buying of accessories is a major problem for most people. You go to the lake and see someone on jet skis, and you can't help but think how much fun it would be to have a pair for yourself. So you buy a pair and use them a couple of times a year.

The problem is obvious. Never buy anything on an impulse. You should consider your options, such as renting. It would make more sense to rent the jet skis for the few times a year you use them. You wouldn't have the debt of buying them or the problem of storing and taking care of them.

Delayed gratification is one of the greatest things in stopping the incurrence of debt. So many young people want everything that they see their parents, or other people who have worked for a long time, have. They fail to realize that these people have spent years accumulating these possessions. It is foolish for young people to think that they should have as much when they are just starting out. It gets even worse when their peers go into debt to buy things. Many people feel they have to keep up with them as well.

Whenever your friends are bragging on something they own, remember that if they didn't pay cash for it, they don't own it.

Please understand I am not saying to pinch pennies like an old tyrant and make yourself miserable in the process. If you want those jet skis very badly, then when you can afford them, by all means, buy them. Quality of life has no price tag. Just be sensible.

The key is to not buy these extras on impulse and go into debt doing it. Also, consider all your options.

Saddling yourself with debt prices perfection into your future. You are making the bet that things will either stay the same or get better so that you can manage the debt. This can cause a great deal of anxiety over the course of the debt payments, and if something happens, as it often does, you will find yourself in a lot of trouble. This happens to many people every year. It is so much easier just to buy things when you can afford them.

The key to being free, not just financially, is having manageable debt.

If your boss comes in and starts becoming, as you believe, unreasonable, your options are limited if you are laden with debt. Some bosses will take advantage of this. When you have been responsible with your money, you have options. You may not want to take one of these options, but it is good to know that you have options if you need them.

One of the best things in this world is to work because you want to, not because you have to. This also makes for better employees. This should be your goal.

I love what I do, but I never want to feel I have to work just for the money. I want to have the option. Managing debt will grant me this peace of mind to know that I go to work because I want to, not because I have to. Managing your debt will do the same for you.

Summary

- **Fix the hole in the boat first, then bail out the water.**

- **You can have when you have.**

- **Look past the door. See the problem, not the symptom.**

- **Own your car.**

- **Life is about the journey, not the destination.**

- **Go to a pub with Johnny South and his wife, Nikki. They are great people. Just don't buy his old car.**

CHAPTER | 4

YOU CAN'T CRASH-DIET— OR CRASH-BUDGET

Start Bailing

You have plugged the leak in the boat. The hardest part is over. You have attacked the problem, however, not the symptom. Now you must decide the best way to bail out the water.

You can't just decide to bail out all the water at once. If that were the case, then no one would be in debt. I don't advocate just working hard. You can train an animal to work hard. What I advocate is not only working hard, but working smart.

You first must develop a systematic debt-reduction plan. Just as you will later develop a systematic savings plan, you will start bailing out your financial water by determining how to rid yourself of debt.

For the first time in your life (for some of you), you will have the ability to walk around in your boat and not get your socks wet.

Setting up a systematic savings and debt-reduction plan is the key to having the option of retiring early. Of course, you will only need your debt-reduction plan until your debt is gone. Some of the happiest people in the world are people that work because they want to—not because they have to. I am not sure I would ever want to retire completely; however, I am positive that I would like that option. Setting up a systematic savings and debt-reduction plan is the only way to have the option of retiring early. Setting up this plan takes a little common sense.

Remember: You can't crash-diet *or* crash-budget.

Start in small amounts if you must, but starting is the key. The way to have a healthier lifestyle for the rest of your life is not to quit all your bad habits at once, which would drive you crazy, but to *slowly* cut out your bad habits. Personally, I would cut out beer last, or at least drink low-calorie whiskey.

To get in shape financially you must first reduce your financial bad habits. You may start slowly, but *start*. Remember, you are preparing yourself for the rest of your life, not just for next week. You can't simply say that from this point forward you will save every extra penny and rid yourself of all debt. You must alter your lifestyle, not just change it dramatically for a short time.

With two good friends, Bruce Prichard and Michael Hayes, one of the original Freebirds—one of the great teams of all time. Bobby and I beat them, though.

Bruce and My Ancestors

In late 2000 I was rummaging through the candy box in the production office during a WWE television show taping. As bad luck would have it, Vince McMahon and Bruce Prichard (one of the WWE vice presidents) were visiting nearby. I walked up to them while unwrapping a piece of candy.

Bruce watched me open the candy and said, "I guess you haven't been told yet."

I knew right away what he was talking about. I knew right

away that *someone* should have talked to me about losing weight. There I was, opening a piece of candy in front of one of my bosses *and* the owner of the company. What great timing. I knew I had gained weight. I had gotten lazy with my diet and workout habits. I just hadn't truly decided what was important.

I knew I had gotten overweight, but I still didn't agree with Bruce when he called me a fat $@&*#. After all, Bruce didn't know my parents, so how could he know if I was a $@&*#? I realized I had gotten fat, but I really didn't think I was a $@&*#. Bruce was the one who had originally called me in Europe to offer me a tryout. He also has been one of my best friends in the company, so I appreciated him telling me I was overweight. If anybody would know if I was a $@&*# or not, it would be Bruce. But I still didn't think I was.

I had a choice to make. I could keep being lazy, or I could get into shape and keep collecting a check. I decided that I really enjoyed getting a check every Monday more than I liked eating candy. Now came the problem.

Altered Lifestyle, Not a Temporary Diet

Bad habits had caused me to become overweight. I needed to change those bad habits. But remember, I believe that life is about living. So I had to find a medium with which I would be happy and still lose weight permanently so I could keep my job.

The main thing I realized was that crash-dieting does not work. For the first time in my life, dieting was necessary. I had watched others go crazy with unhealthy diets that would not work long-term. So I simply cut down. I didn't cut things *out,* I just cut down. And I lost weight.

I wanted to lose weight permanently, not quickly drop thirty pounds in a couple of months, only to gain it back later. I had to alter my lifestyle conclusively. I plan to wrestle several more years, and the older I get, the harder it will be to lose weight. I had to find a way to lose weight and keep it off, especially since fat wrestlers don't look very good on television. As it turned out, the diet alterations were minor.

I knew that the only way to be successful was to determine a way to stay happy with myself, but yet change enough to get into better physical shape. I had to choose the least painful thing to eliminate first.

It was late-night eating.

I cut out the late-night meals and found I really didn't miss them, plus I slept better. I started cutting down on Cokes and candy, something I consumed in excess. I found I didn't miss them much either.

After these two things, I simply began to eat better with each meal. Now understand, I said I cut down on things and I ate better. There are still times I binge on things if I am really craving junk food, but I don't do it as often. I want to lose weight and stay lean—at least until I get through wrestling. That will be several years. You can't crash-diet for several years, but you can do what I am doing.

When I am through wrestling, I may get fat. In fact, I plan to get so fat that I will need large keys on my remote control so I can change the channel.

The main thing I realized was that it had taken me a couple of years of bad habits to get to where I was physically. It would be foolish to think I could take off the weight in a month or so.

I understood that systematically cutting a few things out would have great long-term benefits. For instance, if I cut out one 20-ounce Coke a day (I was drinking several per day), that would equal about 250 calories I would be eliminating daily. This didn't seem like much until I realized how much that one Coke a day added up over a period of time.

If I cut 250 calories a day from my diet, then over a week I would have cut 1,750 calories (7 days × 250 calories = 1,750 calories). This worked out to a pound every two weeks. (There are 3,500 calories in a pound.) Over the course of a year (fifty-two weeks) this would be more than twenty-six pounds I could lose, just by cutting out one Coke a day. Now this small amount started meaning something to me. I also understood that this was not going crazy on a diet, but rather being sensible about what I had to do. This made a lot more sense to me than going on some new-fashioned diet that I would hate.

Change Won't Happen Overnight

It is the same thing with saving and spending habits. You can't go crazy and try to change everything at once. You need to be reasonable about things and start cutting unnecessary things out first. If you are not where you want to be financially and you have developed habits that have put you in this state, then it is silly to think you can change your status overnight. You would go crazy trying. You didn't get in your financial predicament overnight. You can't get out of it overnight, either.

You have to choose to alter your lifestyle. It is the only way to become financially independent. Believe me, this is much better than crash-dieting financially. You can live your life now, and plan for the future, without making yourself miserable. When you are talking about doing things long-term, the things you must do can seem minor. The main thing is to be consistent.

Remember, a consistent, long-term approach means that the small things add up, allowing you to live comfortably now.

You are on the verge of getting the water out of the boat.

You cannot become a very discriminating eater overnight after years of terrible eating habits. You cannot expect to alter your financial lifestyle dramatically, either. But you *are* altering your lifestyle. I don't believe in diets, but I knew I had to lose weight. I decided to change my lifestyle so that becoming over-weight wouldn't happen to me again. A person who diets like crazy and cuts out everything that is bad for them will end up gaining their weight back. In the same way, people that choose to watch their money very tightly for a period of time and then become lax on what they spend will end up in debt again.

As we discussed in chapter 3, I believe that people who have spending and debt problems will not be helped permanently if someone else pays off their debt. Eliminating their debt will only help them for a short time.

The problem is the incurrence of debt, not the debt itself. You must alter your lifestyle to address spending and debt problems. Then, and only then, will the debt reduction you have mean any-thing for the long term. It is the same as people that have lipo-suction to rid themselves of excess fat. They are doing nothing about the habits that made them obese. It won't be long until that fat returns, because the problems that created the fat are still there.

You have to find a medium with which you will be happy— one that you will be able to keep for the rest of your life. Find a way to save out of every one of your checks and reduce debt until it is gone. Do not start out by altering your spending habits so dramatically that you will end up unhappy or discouraged. You still have to live, even though you are planning for your future.

New Year's Resolutions

I get a kick every year out of going around the country and watching the New Year's Resolutionists working out. These people have decided that with the dawn of the New Year they are going to turn back the clock and whip themselves into shape. They come in with their gloves and lifting straps and work very hard. I said *hard,* not *smart.* They sweat and groan, usually loudly, and do every exercise known to man.

You can usually put a calendar on these people. By the third week in January, you won't be seeing the New Year's Resolutionists anymore. Of course, next year a new crop will take their place.

The problem is moderation. It took years for some of these couch potatoes to get into such poor shape. Many of them haven't worked out since college or high school. Instead of coming in and slowly getting into shape—goodness knows they slowly got fat—they want to do it all at once.

Bad idea.

If these people would just realize that a healthier lifestyle is an ongoing progression, not a destination you can reach in a matter of weeks, then their outlook would be significantly different. You can't kill yourself to get into good physical shape any more than you can kill yourself to get out of debt and save money. You go to the gym so you will feel better. Working so hard that you get hurt or burned out defeats the purpose. Likewise, saving money and reducing debt makes your life better. Making yourself miserable defeats the purpose.

Since the beginning of the stock market the average stock has returned 11 percent, and bonds have returned about half of that. History has shown that credit card debt interest is higher than both stock and bond returns. The most foolish debt in the world is credit card debt. Credit cards are so easy to use and can so easily get you in a world of financial trouble. They also kill you on the interest charged. Whenever you talk about good debt and bad debt, there can be arguments over certain things. Credit card debt is not one of these things. Credit card debt is bad debt.

You must eliminate credit card debt.

Just as you will have to set up a systematic, regular savings and investing plan, if you are saddled with debt, you will have to set up a regular plan to eliminate that debt. You have already plugged the hole in the boat. Start bailing out the water.

Good Debt vs. Bad Debt

In chapter 3 we began discussing good and bad debt; now it is time to write that debt down. Look at your debt. Now list your debt from bad to good. Start with the worst debt you have, most likely your credit card debt, and then go all the way to your best debt, probably the mortgage on your home. Try this:

Debt Ranking
  1. (Worst debt I have—i.e., credit card debt)
  2.
  3.
  4.
  5. (Best debt I have—i.e., mortgage)

The key to getting out of debt with a realistic plan is to start with your worst debt first and begin to pay it off. Then proceed to your second worst debt and pay it off, then keep going until you are completely debt-free. It is important to realize what debt is unreasonable debt (your worst debt), and to begin to pay it off first. In this way you are being wise about paying off your debt, and you will develop a plan that is efficient and smart. Remember, you have to set your goal first, then work backward.

You may choose at some point not to pay off your mortgage. A lot of financial advisers would recommend this. We will decide later in the book if that is the best choice for you.

Some of your debt you may decide to pay off with a loan payment instead of concentrating on eliminating it slowly. However, your bad debt is something that you will want to pay off first.

You might ask, "Where does this money come from?"

Good question. You have already given yourself a pay cut. This is the first part of the extra money you will use to pay off debt. You now know that you will own your car for ten years. Since you will own it that long, your payments will end. Instead of counting this as extra money, make those payments now toward your debt. You are already accustomed to this expense. Never quit making payments—just make them toward reducing your debt.

Figure out each week or month how much you can put toward debt reduction and savings, and be consistent with this amount.

Okay, let's look at your debt. Where are your highest interest rates? This is the debt you should pay off first. Normally, this is credit card debt.

If you have something higher than credit card debt, then it is probably to a guy named Guido that looks as if he should be on *The Sopranos.* If you have this problem, put the book down and go buy a self-defense book. I think it will come in handy.

Start with the highest rate you are being charged on your debt and determine how much you can start paying each week or each month.

You first have to know the amount of debt you have, and especially the amount of *bad* debt you have. This is where the worksheet in chapter 1 comes in handy (see page 43). You have to decide on a realistic time frame in which to pay off your bad debt. Decide whether you can pay off your debt in a year, two, five, or however many years you need.

Once you know how much debt you are facing, then you can determine how much you can afford to pay weekly or monthly toward reducing that debt. If you have $5,000 in credit card debt and you can afford to pay $100 a month toward that debt, figuring a typical credit card interest rate of 18.5 percent, you would pay off that debt in eight years. Of course, you would pay a total of $9,600, because of the high interest rate, to eliminate a $5,000 debt. Believe me when I tell you, you need to do everything possible to get out of you credit card debt.

Set Your Goals and Work Backward

You need to determine a time frame in which to pay off your debt. I can assure you that if you don't set a goal, you won't reach it. You have to plan a little. It won't be much, but plan enough to know where you are headed and what you are doing with your money. If you don't know what you are doing with your money, then four years from now, you will be no better off than you are now. That is a waste, at least financially, of four years.

You may think that four, five, or more years is a long time to pay off your debt. Remember, you didn't get in your financial predicament overnight. You won't be debt-free overnight either. If you don't start reducing your current debt, however slowly, you will never be better off. You have to play the cards dealt to you in the best possible way. Sometimes you will like the cards, sometimes you won't. It doesn't matter. You can't gripe about the cards; there is never any sense griping about something you can't change. The only option is to decide the best way to play the cards.

You first have to have quit incurring debt, so each month your debt should be getting smaller. This is an enjoyable thing to watch. Instead of dreading your monthly bills, you will start looking forward to seeing them, because your debt will be smaller each month. The bottom line on the worksheet in chapter 1 should be growing each month, because your debt will be shrinking and your savings will be growing. This is a great indicator that you are heading the right direction.

Is Mick Cheap or Frugal?

Creative thinking often helps stop the incurrence of debt. Mick Foley allegedly used this creative thinking process during a stay in New York. I say "allegedly" because Mick never completely owned up to the story.

Mick Foley and I in Oman on a wrestling tour to the UAE.

We often stayed in the Holiday Inn by the Newark Airport while working in New York. Normally it would be a very late night getting out of Madison Square Garden and back to Newark. Almost all the guys would have very early flights home. It generally made for a few hours of sleep or a few hours at the bar, a shower, and a rush to the airport. We would get back to the hotel around midnight or later. Often we would have flights as early as five or six o'clock in the morning, making a rather short night.

Mick was spotted a couple of times very late at night sitting in the lobby reading a paper. We later accused him, I believe correctly (Mick was known for his frugality—or rather cheapness), of pretending to read the paper so he wouldn't have to pay for a room. Later he would catch an early flight home.

Mick claimed this wasn't exactly true, but rather the hotel was sold out.

I always believed that Mick had found a new way of stopping the incurrence of debt.

Mick has been a good friend of mine. He was the first to recommend me to several people in the financial world for interviews, for which I am very grateful. However, I still think he was there reading a paper to avoiding paying for a room.

If you are employing this type of creative thinking, I want you to know that your motives are good, but a little misguided.

Establishing a Debt-Elimination Plan

Once you have decided which debt is costing you the most, establish a plan for abolishing it. Understand that if you owe $1,000 and the interest on that each month is $15, then if you only send in $15, you won't be making any headway. Of course, you won't be losing ground either, which is better than not paying at all. You have to be able to pay in to the principal, which in this case is the $1,000. The worst thing in the world for people trying to get out of debt is only making the minimum payment amount on credit cards. *This minimum payment amount assures that you owe the credit card company forever.* These people don't want you to pay off your debt. They are making too much money off consumers to want that. Credit card companies want you to carry a debt load each month so that they can charge their high interest rates to debt-laden consumers.

If you have debt that has high interest rates, that is where you should concentrate. I would still be saving a little while you are paying off that debt, however. It is a great confidence builder to see your savings growing as you are paying off your debt. It shows that you are doing the right thing. There is no feeling like knowing that you are making your future better.

If you work for a large company, then you are probably already saving in your 401(k) or similar retirement plan. You must max out your payment to this account. There are some 401(k)s that allow after-tax contributions; make sure that if yours does, you put your money in pre-tax. How you diversify in this account we will discuss later. It is important to be saving for retirement while you are paying off your debt, for several reasons, that we will discuss later, not to mention psychologically. Seeing your retirement account go up is a terrific confidence booster—it shows you that you are making your future better.

Shaka Zulu and Two Dumb Cowboys

Sometimes it is just important to be headed in the right direction. In 1996, I was with WWE in South Africa on a wrestling tour. Barry Windham and I decided to go to where they had filmed *Shaka Zulu*. We rented a car and asked directions. The problem was our English.

We started driving, and driving, and driving. We soon realized that we had not seen any tourists for a long time. In fact, we had not seen any white people for a long time. In fact, the black people were either really good character actors, or else we were in Zulu tribal land.

We were in Zulu tribal land.

When we finally made sense of the map, we realized we were deep into Zulu land, and the tribe was not known to be too peaceful at the time. We didn't have much chance of fitting in, either.

We followed the map in the direction we thought we were told to go and realized that we had gone not to a TV set but to an actual Zulu village—perhaps Shaka's actual home, I don't know. It looked like something out of a Tarzan movie, except no popcorn.

Soon our car was surrounded. We got out, with our cowboy hats on, to incredulous looks. I can just imagine they were just as shocked to see us as we were. The people were very nice, even showed us one of their dances that was going on. The problem was, it was getting dark, and to be quite honest I didn't know what or who was for dinner.

After the main guy, we met the chief. After the tribe members tried on our hats, we finally convinced them to let us leave. We needed a plan. We decided that if we had a flat tire at this time of night, we were just going to keep driving.

I didn't say it was a good plan, but you have to start somewhere.

The farther we got from the village, the more confidence we attained. It is usually that way when you are getting yourself out of trouble. Needless to say, we did make it back. What a joy it was when we finally realized we were headed in the right direction and that we were going to make it.

How Much Can You Spare?

Generally it is a good idea to determine how much of your salary you can put toward either reducing debt or increasing savings. Five to 10 percent is a good place to start. If you start at 10 percent, and you are both reducing debt and increasing your retirement, split up the money either equally or however you see fit.

After you have paid off all of your high-interest debt, then it is good to look at your other debt. A mortgage on your house isn't always the best thing to pay off because you get a tax break on the interest portion of your payments, and typically interest on a house payment isn't too high. Most mortgages have relatively low interest rates, but it is also important to know that interest you pay on your mortgage is tax-deductible. Not only are you paying a relatively low interest rate, you get a tax break that lowers the effective interest cost after the payment of income taxes even further. Generally, you will make more money by investing that money instead of paying off your house.

I had a mortgage on which I was being charged 7 percent. Because of the tax break on interest, I was only losing around 4 to 5 percent on my money. There are not too many investments that won't make you at least 5 percent annually. So if you pay off your mortgage with money you could be investing elsewhere, then theoretically and technically, you lose money.

If you have a mortgage that is at 7 percent and you are in the 27 percent tax bracket, then the amount you are losing on your money is actually 5.1 percent, because you get a tax deduction on the interest you pay on your mortgage. If you have an investment that is making more than 5.1 percent, then you are losing money by paying off your mortgage—technically. I say *technically* because there is an unquantifiable amount of peace of mind that some people gain from owning their house outright. That peace of mind can't be measured in a percentage.

However, each person is different, and if paying off your house will give you peace of mind, then once you have paid off all of your higher interest debt, start paying off your house. It is a great feeling to pay off your house, one that very few people these days get to feel.

Remember, this is *your* life; if you want to pay off something different first, feel free to do it. If you have a debt that bothers you, for whatever reason, then start with that. Maybe you hate going into your local bank knowing you owe them money. If this is the case, then pay off the bank first. As long as you're paying off your debt, you will not be doing the wrong thing.

Each individual is different. That is what makes this world so good. That is also what makes a uniform way of doing things worthless. The importance you put on things will vary from how I feel. For that reason, once you have paid off the majority of your debt, and you have just your house and a car payment left, you must decide what will make your life better. Car interest payments can be extremely low, much lower than you would make investing your money. Technically, you would be losing money by paying off something with such a small interest rate. Peace of mind has no price tag, though, and it definitely is not the wrong thing to pay off your debt.

I think it is wiser to start with your highest interest rate debt and pay it off first; then use the money you set aside to pay that debt on your next highest interest rate debt until you are debt-free.

Personally, as they say in West Texas, I like to *owe nothing to no one.* I believe that if I own my house and don't owe anything, then I can always pay to keep the lights on in my house by pumping gas if necessary. The only problem with that is that there are no full-service gas stations here in my hometown of Athens, Texas. I do have a lawn mower, though. People always need their grass trimmed.

I believe in delayed gratification, but you must be reasonable.

Teddy "Don't Look at Me at a Tollbooth" Long

Ron Simmons and I normally travel together between towns. Occasionally other guys will split the car rental with us. Normally, it is either the Godfather (Charles Wright) or Teddy Long (Teddy Long). Teddy is so tight, I believe he still has some Confederate money in his deep pockets. He wouldn't know that, though, because his alligator arms don't allow him to get to the bottom of his pockets.

Me, Teddy Long, and Ron Simmons at a *WrestleMania* party. Teddy did not pay for the drink in his hand.

We believe Teddy is a direct descendant of the astronomer Galileo. Every time we go through a tollbooth, Teddy is busy gazing at the stars and not reaching into his deep pockets. I am sure that over the course of time he will have neck problems because of this.

Now this is definitely one way of not going into debt; however, you could end up spending the money you save on a chiropractor. I believe you could imitate Teddy in moderation, such as studying the stars at alternate tollbooths.

I wouldn't say Teddy is cheap—he would have to spend more

money to be cheap. Teddy is in his own league. But since we like him, he will always be welcome to ride with us. We just know not to bother him while we are going through a tollbooth. Maybe he is secretly working for NASA. Remember, be reasonable. It is okay to pay for your share of tolls.

Two White Guys Living in the Hood

Once you have found a good, sound debt-reduction policy, then you should find a way to start saving money in the same systematic fashion. However, it is important to save money in a way that you will not have ready access to it.

Bobby Duncum Jr. was one of my first tag team partners in wrestling. We lived together in Dallas in a pretty rough community. It was one of those places where they check you for weapons at the gate, and if you don't have any, they will lend you one. Actually, we didn't have a gate. It probably had been stolen. Okay, it wasn't that bad, but we did hear gunshots occasionally—every Friday night. We would have had to cross the tracks just to get to the bad side of town. We were way past the bad side—I think we were in a war zone.

Bobby was a terrific, easygoing guy. That was his downfall with money. If Bobby had money, he spent it. Bobby was getting money from the Arena Football League weekly because of a settlement due to an injury. Neither one of us was making enough money to live very well, so Bobby always offered to pay for things. The problem was that Bobby didn't mind paying for everybody. Bobby was just too nice.

We both knew that Bobby wouldn't be getting the settlement checks much longer. We knew he needed to save some money, or else when the well ran dry, he would have nothing to show for the money he had earned. Remember, I had already learned the hard way about having nothing to show for your money. It is amazing how the best lessons are learned the hard way. This is one of the reasons I am writing this book, so that you won't have to learn the hard way as well.

Believe me, the hard way stinks.

Bobby set up a savings account that was not accessible by an ATM card. We learned that in his situation inaccessibility was a very important aspect of saving money. This way, no matter how much he wanted money on the weekend, he couldn't get it until Monday when the bank opened. The temptation was just too great late at night or on the weekend to withdraw money and spend it. Bobby solved his problem by not allowing himself accessibility to his money. He ended up saving a lot of money this way.

It is just too easy and tempting to get money out of an account when you think you need it. For this reason I suggest that you save money in a way that doesn't let you touch it very easily. That way, when the last call is made, you won't be able to access your savings.

It is simply too easy to withdraw money saved over the course of time in a savings account for some unexpected spending. It is also very easy to justify this type of spending. Whenever something goes wrong with your house or car and you have money saved, it is too easy to rationalize an expenditure. The problem then is that you have spent all your savings, and you are back to square one.

The solution is to find an alternative way to pay off the emergency debt—get a cheap loan or sell your bass boat. Once you realize that your savings and retirement is something you cannot touch, then you will find a way to pay for emergencies. Don't touch your retirement.

It is amazing how people always find money for the things that are important to them. If your air conditioning goes out in your house in the summer, you will find a way to fix it. If you have put your money that you are investing in a place that is hard to retrieve, you will not be as tempted to try. You will find a way to get the extra money you need without spending your retirement. When you save money, consider it gone and untouchable, or you will be tempted to spend it. There will always be an important reason to spend it if you don't.

You must decide that the money you put toward your future is money that will be used for your future. Believe me, once you get used to the fact that a certain portion of your check will go toward savings, you will adjust and live within your means.

Think about how much extra money you could save a month. How about just $50? Now if you agreed to that, then I want you to hand this book to a friend and ask him to take three paces back. Then have him turn around and throw the book, hitting you between the eyes. Now wipe off the blood. Fifty dollars? That is one meal at a decent restaurant, one trip to a movie with your family, or one ticket to an NBA basketball game. (Wrestling tickets are cheaper, and you get better entertainment anyway.) Let's say you can save $50 a week. Some of you will be able to save more, and some of you will be able to save less. For the sake of an example we'll use $50 a week.

This may not sound like much, so let's see how much you will accrue over a year. Over the course of one year, you will have saved (without any interest you would have earned on your money figured into the equation) $2,600. Not bad. However, it gets much better.

Compounding interest is one of the great things about saving money long-term. You are about to see why.

Why Compounding Interest Is So Good

The average equity (stock) has produced over the history of the stock market an 11 percent return annually. There have been down times (bear markets), and there have been good times (bull markets), but on average, the stock market has produced 11 percent gains. Since this is the average gain, we will use this figure to show how compounding interest works in your favor.

If you save $2,600 per year for ten years, and you achieve the average return on your money of 11 percent, after ten years you will have $43,477.22. That's not bad at all. Time is in your favor with compounding interest.

If you save the same amount for twenty years, again with the average return of 11 percent, you will have $166,927.36. Now say that you have saved this same amount for thirty years, with all the same criteria, and then you will have saved, with compounding interest, $517,454.27. Now you are able to talk about retiring well off on just $50 a week.

The key is consistent savings.

Another great thing about owning stock is that all of the return you get until you sell your stock is not taxed, so it grows interest-free. If your stock grows at an average rate of 11 percent annually, then that 11 percent is not taxed until you sell that stock. Because there is a long-term capital gains tax in the United States right now, if you hold the stock a minimum of twelve months, you will only pay 20 percent tax on the profits instead of your normal tax rate. Long-term capital gains means simply that if you hold an equity (stock) twelve months or longer, it is considered long-term. The tax rate for this long-term gain is only 20 percent, and Congress is trying to lower that rate.

The great part about this is that if you don't sell, you don't pay tax.

There will be times when you receive a lump sum of money. You may either pay off a great deal of your debt or substantially increase your savings. This is a great thing to do; however, over the long term the key to saving a lot of money is consistency.

Dollar-Cost Averaging

Dollar-cost averaging is the best way to invest. Dollar-cost averaging is investing the same amount each week or month. This helps avoid any market fluctuations and having to time the market. This way, when you are investing in a stock or mutual fund, you don't have to worry about trying to find a good buy point. When the stock or mutual fund price is low, you will get more shares of it that month. When the price is high, you will get fewer shares. Over the course of time, you will end up buying at a good average price.

Too many people try to time the market with the money they are investing. This is something the professionals have a hard—if not impossible—time doing. The old adage is true.

It is *time in the market* that is important, not *timing the market.*

By consistently investing the same amount of money, you avoid analyzing stock or fund prices daily.

Investing regularly is the best way to invest, whether it is through a company plan such as a 401(k) or on your own.

However, invest in a good, solid plan where you can't withdraw the money easily. While depositing money in a savings account is better than not saving anything, it is not the best thing to do. First, you will not get a great interest rate. Second, it is too easy to get your money out to buy something you want.

Once you start saving money on a regular basis, you will find that you can increase the amount of money you will save, because you will find out you aren't missing the money you set aside each week.

Remember That Pay Cut?

If you are making $50,000 a year and your boss told you he was going to lower your salary by 5 percent, you would adjust and it would not have a huge impact on your life. Saving 5 or 10 percent out of your paycheck is something to which you will adjust easily.

Odds are, you have never been homeless and on the street or starved for a bite to eat. Odds are also that you have not always made the amount of money you make now. Whether higher or lower, you probably have had to operate on different salaries. How did you do it? I have lived off a wide range of income levels.

Cindy and I have lived off very little and have been fortunate to live off a decent salary. Looking back, we never went hungry or missed doing something we wanted. Now we might have stayed or lived in better places, but we still lived just fine. My point is you adapt to whatever your circumstances are.

I find it very sad that some people in our society go through so much money and end up with virtually nothing. You have to ask how these people could go through millions of dollars and not have anything to show for their money. It is even more amazing to realize that these people once lived on a whole lot less before they became rich. You would think that they would be able to save their money when they started making a lot more.

The problem is habits.

They spent more than they made when they made very little, and now they spend more than they make while they are making a lot.

You first must correct your bad financial habits, or it won't matter how much money you make. You have to plug the leak in the boat, or no matter how big the boat is, you will always take on water.

A Good Economics Test

I would dare to say that if you take a person that lives within his means and saves money regularly, and you give all of his money to a person who lives way past his means and has never been successful at saving, an interesting thing would happen. Within ten years the first person would have overcome his loss of savings and again have money in the bank. The second person would have blown all the money and be in debt again. I think that is a safe bet. The debt isn't the problem—it is only a symptom. You don't get rid of the problem permanently by treating the symptom. The problem is the problem. (How is that for good English?) Treat the problem, not the symptom.

If you are making a lot of money, you adapt to that higher income. If you are making very little, you adapt to the lower income. When you start saving on a systematic plan, or start reducing your debt on a systematic plan, you will grow accustomed to the minute change in take-home pay. You have every time in the past; you will this time too. This is why it is important to be reasonable about how you intend to change your habits to start saving money. It has to be something with which you can live. Remember, I am talking not about a quick fix, but a permanent fix.

This is why I believe in living your life enjoyably. Don't make yourself miserable saving for the future. There *is* a happy medium. The only way for a permanent fix is to find a way to save that doesn't affect your lifestyle in a significant way.

Saving systematically is the key.

Summary

- The greatest invention of modern man is compounding interest.

- Dollar-cost averaging—investing the same amount each week or month—is the best way to invest.

- Time in the market is much more important than timing the market.

- You must alter your lifestyle to expect long-term results. Quick fixes don't work.

- Pay off your highest-interest debt first.

- If you are overweight, don't be seen eating candy by Bruce Prichard. He will insult your ancestry.

- Don't look for Teddy to pay at a tollbooth.

CHAPTER | 5

REASONS TO INVEST

Take Off the Hubcap

Most companies—as well as the federal government—go out of their way to encourage savings. In the past couple of years, the government has revised its tax laws so extensively that it makes it foolish not to take advantage of the tax breaks afforded to every citizen. Government-sponsored tax savings plans and company-sponsored 401(k) plans have made it not only easier to save money, but also extremely beneficial.

It is no crime to look for ways to pay less taxes. The law books that levy taxes on you are the same law books that give the ways to pay less. You just must be willing to do a little research.

Korean Wieners and Asian Taxes

Wrestling in Korea taught me firsthand about taxes. My good friend and roommate, Bobby Duncum Jr., and I had spent two weeks in Korea in what I would describe as less than ideal conditions. Not that we were not taken care of by Mr. Pyong—we were—we just spoke no Korean and had a hard time getting along. We spent the first week griping about the only food we could find—wieners from a local convenience store. Once we tried to boil them in our hotel coffeemaker, we realized that the wieners were individually wrapped in plastic. They tasted much better without the plastic coating.

After two horrible weeks of plastic-wiener eating and climbing out dressing room windows to get away from avid Korean wrestling fans, we were finally going home. All that remained was picking up my paycheck. Interestingly, we were paid 80 percent of our salary because 20 percent was taken out for "new taxes," according to our Asian promoter (not the Koreans). Amazingly, his English got much worse when we asked for our money. It seemed like a strange coincidence that almost exactly 20 percent of the shows were canceled also.

I can't do anything about dishonest Asian promoters or horrible plastic-coated Korean wieners (actually Bobby and I both referred to the promoter as a wiener, though in a slightly different term), but your taxes here in the United States can be cut with a little planning.

Any money you can save in a tax deduction is money that you have earned. For instance, if you are in the 25 percent tax bracket (if your adjusted gross income is over $46,700, then you would pay 27 percent on the amount over $46,700, in addition to a base of $6,405), then whatever money on which you can save paying taxes will instantly make you that 25 percent. For example, if you make a $100 deduction on your taxes, then you have earned that $25 you would have owed the government. A 25 percent instant return on your money is not a bad return.

One of the main problems with the tax savings plans from the government and the 401(k) plans offered by companies is that at first (and sometimes second) glance, they appear to be very complicated.

The key is to take off the hubcap. Look past the door.

Tom "Why Is That Ditch in the Road?" Prichard

In 1996, my first full year with WWE, business was not very good. In fact, there were some arenas in which you could have shot a gun and not hit anybody—nobody was there. There was a real lull period when WWE was shifting its business paradigm from a character-oriented business to a more modern, story-line-motivated business.

Now don't get me wrong. The creation of several characters helped business greatly—Steve Austin, The Rock, Triple H, Burt Angle (I know his name is misspelled, but he misspelled my name in his book, and I still have a little childish vengeful attitude), and, of course, Undertaker, to mention just a few. These guys carry the main event every single night and do a great job.

The day we went to war with Afghanistan, toasting our soldiers. We had an impromptu "Bomba Osama" party; unfortunately, Burt Ankle (yes, I spelled it wrong) brought the refreshments: milk. Ron, Burt, me, Edge, Stone Cold, and Matt Hardy.

However, when I first joined WWE in December of 1995, these guys, with the exception of Undertaker (who had been the cornerstone of the company for over a decade, and still is), had not emerged. This was still a while before Steve would win *King of the Ring* and usher in a new era for WWE.

Business was bad.

Because business was so bad, I usually split a room with at least two guys to lower costs. Normally these two guys were Tom Prichard and Dutch Mantel. We also split the cost of a rental car.

We three wise men were driving one foggy night between Allentown, Pennsylvania, and Newark, New Jersey, when I realized that I could not see the road. I was certainly glad Tom Prichard was driving, because he seemed to be able to see the road just fine.

Tom is a real first-class individual, but his driving skills lack something—such as skill. In fact, in the history of the automobile Tom may be the worst driver ever to have driven. I don't know how Dutch drives, because he never drove; however, he did keep me awake with some of the best storytelling I had ever heard. And, like Teddy, he never paid tolls either.

Quite a contrast: Tom Prichard (the worst driver in the history of the automobile) and Hermie Sadler (a NASCAR driver—he built the motor in my blue truck), along with Hermie's wife, Angie, and Cindy.

You might ask why we let Tom drive, to which I would answer, "I don't know." This particular night he seemed to be doing fine. Tom was clipping along at about 70 mph when he looked at me and said, "You know, I can't see a thing." I would say this scared me, but *terrified* is more accurate.

I asked Tom if he would like to slow down, and he looked at me (which was okay, because he certainly couldn't see the road) and asked if I was scared. I told him, "No, I am way past scared."

Now, depending on whose story you believe—the truth or Tom's version—the next part becomes very interesting. According to Tom, there was a ditch in the middle of a major four-lane highway that he ran headlong into. According to Dutch and me, Tom ran off the road and almost killed us while he was asking if I was scared.

I have never seen a ditch in the middle of a highway. But since that night I couldn't even see past the hood of the car, I will give Tom the benefit of the doubt.

What happened next is indisputable. Tom hit the ditch so

hard, he blew out the front tire. When we made it back onto the road (again on the presumption that the ditch was where most ditches are, not in the middle of the road), we pulled over to change it.

I retrieved the little toy jack that comes with these new cars and started jacking up the car. Tom was trying to loosen the lug nuts. Suddenly, Tom proclaimed that the bolts were stripped. Dutch gave it a try; then he, too, proclaimed that the bolts were stripped.

When I finally got through with the jack, I looked at the tire, then at Dutch and Tom, sitting on the side of the road. I asked them to point out which bolts were stripped. They stated that all of them were. I then proceeded to berate them for the next few seconds, explaining that if they would take off the hubcap, they would get to the real lug nuts. They had tried to take the fake nuts off of the hubcap.

If these two were the pit crew for Dale Earnhardt, Earnhardt would have never won a race and probably would have gotten lost in the pit area trying to find his way back on to the track. Dutch later asked me not to tell anybody, so I agreed that I wouldn't. So if you see Dutch, don't tell him that this story is in my book, because Dutch and Tom both are still my good friends.

Deciphering the difference between the savings in a company 401(k) and the government tax incentives can seem a daunting task.

The key is to take off the hubcap.

When I removed the hubcap from the rental car wheel, the solution (the nuts and bolts) became very easy and clear. It just took a little extra looking.

It is exactly the same with these tax-deductible savings plans. A little looking reveals that deciphering the best plan for you is not that complicated. Actually, when you break it down into the component parts of a savings plan, it is very easy. You don't need to know the whole tax book, just what affects you.

Please understand, though, that some of the dumbest thinking comes when people think they need to spend money for a tax deduction. This is the same thinking that people implement when they buy things on sale. These savvy shoppers believe they saved 25 percent on a sale purchase, but in reality, they still had to spend the other 75 percent to make the purchase. If the product is something that you needed anyway and you waited until it went on sale to buy it, then you have been a wise consumer. If you simply bought something just because it was on sale, then you wasted money.

Just because elephants are two for $10 does not mean you are making a great deal. It's only a good deal *if* you have $10 and *if* you need two elephants.

I hate to hear people say that they bought something for the sole reason that it was a tax deduction. You are better off saving the 75 percent now than the 25 percent come tax time. You should strive to save money on taxes, but the main thing is to worry about making money first. You do not make money by spending it on things you don't need just because it is a tax deduction.

There are numerous ways to lower your taxes legally. I don't like paying taxes any more than you do, but I like jail even less. For peace of mind and because it is the right thing to do, I would advise strongly against being "creative" on your taxes.

Isn't it amazing what kind words we put on things when we are really just cheating?

IRAs

Two of the greatest investment vehicles, which everyone that has the opportunity should be involved in, are the different IRAs and the 401(k). If you want to have the ability to choose to work or not work, then you should take full advantage of all of the retirement plans available. If you are going to get a tax break and/or matching funds from your company, you should consider these plans mandatory.

Every year the government is doing things that benefit the taxpayer. The Roth IRA is one of the latest creations, and one of the best.

The Roth IRA

The Taxpayer Relief Act of 1997 created the Roth IRA, and it has become one of the greatest tax-free investment vehicles the government has invented.

With the Roth IRA, in 2003 you may put up to $3,000 in a retirement account. The money is not deductible in the year in which you deposit it, but is completely tax-free when you take it out. The traditional IRA is deductible the same year you make the contribution; however, it is taxed when it is withdrawn.

If you are married and filing jointly, you are eligible to contribute the full amount to a Roth IRA if your adjusted gross income (AGI) is below $150,000, at which point the benefits start phasing out until you hit $160,000.

If you are married and filing jointly, and your AGI is above $160,000, you can skip this part because you do not qualify to contribute to the Roth IRA.

If you are single filing alone, you are eligible for a Roth IRA if your AGI is below $95,000. The benefits start phasing out at $95,000.00 until you reach $110,000.

If you are single filing alone, and you make over $110,000, you can quit reading this part because you don't qualify to contribute.

The contributions allowable for the Roth IRA start going up in subsequent years, and they are greater for those over fifty years of age.

Roth IRA Contribution Levels

		Over 50
2003	$3,000	$3,500
2004	$3,000	$3,500
2005	$4,000	$4,500
2006	$4,000	$5,000

If you are currently involved in a company retirement plan, then you are only allowed to contribute to a Roth IRA if your AGI is below $150,000 (married filing jointly) or $95,000 (single filing alone). The traditional IRA levels are much lower. If you are married and filing jointly, you can contribute the full amount up to $53,999, and that is phased out at $64,000. If you are single filing alone, you can contribute the full amount if your AGI is below $33,999, and that amount is phased out at $44,000.

Most people, when first given the opportunity to save money now or save down the road, will believe that their best option is to take the money now instead of later. It is not necessarily greed that drives this; it just seems like a better deal. The reason they believe this is because they have never looked long-term at what they could save with compounding interest.

The whole key is to take off the hubcap.

Benefits of the Roth IRA

When you understand the effect of compounding interest, then you understand that the $3,000 you initially deposit can become quite a large sum. If you were to put this $3,000 into an account that earned you 8 percent interest over the course of thirty years, then this initial investment would have grown into $30,179.97. Now remember the average stock historically has returned an average of 11 to 12 percent, and we are only using an 8 percent return. This sum of $30,179.97 would be completely tax-free.

Another good thing about the Roth IRA is that you can withdraw up to $10,000 early, with no penalty, to buy a home. You can also withdraw early if you have become disabled.

If you are still fairly young, then the Roth IRA is probably best for you. Simply put, if you have enough time that the money will double (the rule of 72, see page 124) or more, then the Roth IRA is the plan that will benefit you the most. Remember that the ini-

Rule of Seventy-Two

The rule of 72, a mathematical rule that shows how quickly money can double with different interest rates, is a very simple way of showing how compounding interest works.

To apply the rule of 72, take the interest rate you have and divide it into 72. The result is how long it will take for your money to double. If you have a 7 percent interest rate, your money will double in approximately ten years, because you have divided 7 into 72 and gotten approximately 10 and some change. If your interest rate is 10 percent, your money will double about every seven years (72 divided by 10 gives you about 7).

Here is the good part. If you achieve an average return on the stock market of approximately 11 percent, your money will double about every six to seven years. So, if you have $5,000 to start with, in seven years it will have doubled to $10,000. Seven more years, and it doubles again to $20,000. Seven more, it doubles to $40,000. In twenty-one years, $5,000 has become $40,000.

*The rule of 72 is a very simple way to figure return on your investments.

tial $3,000 investment is not tax-free. If you have a lengthy time frame, such as ten years or more, then the Roth IRA is for you. In the example, the $3,000 is still taxed, but $27,179.97 you earned from your investment is completely tax-free. That is a pretty good deal. It is also a deal that you are not very wise if you don't take advantage of.

This is how much your initial investment would grow if you had an 8 percent return. The average stock has historically returned around 11 percent. If you had an 11 percent return, then that amount would have grown into $68,676.69.

You can see why it is so important to get as much return as possible. Those extra three percentage points gave you an additional $38,000 in savings. You still pay tax on the original $3,000, but the rest of the $65,676.69 is tax-free.

This example is just from one year investing and letting that money grow. You should be investing each year, and then you will see how well you will be able to live when you retire. If you were to invest $3,000 each year for the rest of those thirty years, with the same return of 8 percent, you would have $309,661.66 in your Roth account.

So while you paid tax initially every year on the $3,000 you invest, this means that you paid tax on a total of $90,000 (30 years × $3,000 = $90,000). The rest of that amount, $219,661.66, is completely tax-free. What a deal.

Your Roth IRA compounds tax-free for all the years it is in your retirement account and is also tax-free upon withdrawal. You should write Mr. Roth a thank-you note.

If you were to get the average return of the stock market, which is 11 percent, the returns start to become phenomenal. If you contribute $3,000 annually for thirty years, you would end up with $662,740 tax-free.

What follows is a simple spreadsheet that shows how compounding interest works with 11 percent interest.

Investing $3,000 per Year at 11 Percent Interest

Year	Investment	Start Year	Year-End Interest	Year-End Total
1	$3,000	$3,000	$330	$3,330
2	$3,000	$6,330	$696	$7,026
3	$3,000	$10,026	$1,103	$11,129
4	$3,000	$14,129	$1,554	$15,683
5	$3,000	$18,683	$2,055	$20,739
6	$3,000	$23,739	$2,611	$26,350
7	$3,000	$29,350	$3,228	$32,578
8	$3,000	$35,578	$3,914	$39,492
9	$3,000	$42,492	$4,674	$47,166
10	$3,000	$50,166	$5,518	$55,684
11	$3,000	$58,684	$6,455	$65,140
12	$3,000	$68,140	$7,495	$75,635
13	$3,000	$78,635	$8,650	$87,285
14	$3,000	$90,285	$9,931	$100,216
15	$3,000	$103,216	$11,354	$114,570
16	$3,000	$117,570	$12,933	$130,503
17	$3,000	$133,503	$14,685	$148,188
18	$3,000	$151,188	$16,631	$167,818
19	$3,000	$170,818	$18,790	$189,608
20	$3,000	$192,608	$21,187	$213,795
21	$3,000	$216,795	$23,847	$240,643
22	$3,000	$243,643	$26,801	$270,444
23	$3,000	$273,444	$30,079	$303,522
24	$3,000	$306,522	$33,717	$340,240
25	$3,000	$343,240	$37,756	$380,996
26	$3,000	$383,966	$42,240	$426,236
27	$3,000	$429,236	$47,216	$476,452
28	$3,000	$479,452	$52,740	$532,192
29	$3,000	$535,192	$58,871	$594,063
30	$3,000	$597,063	$65,677	$662,740

Investing the same $3,000 per year but with different interest rates would give you:

	5%	8%	11%
5 years	$17,406	$19,008	$20,739
10 years	$39,620	$46,936	$55,684
15 years	$67,972	$87,973	$114,570
20 years	$104,158	$148,269	$213,795
25 years	$150,340	$236,863	$380,996
30 years	$209,282	$367,038	$662,740

Another good thing about the IRAs is that you are allowed to trade assets in your retirement account with no penalty.

Also, with the Roth IRA you do not have to withdraw the money at age seventy (as in a traditional IRA). You may leave the money in the Roth until you die. You may start withdrawing tax-free at age fifty-nine.

These tax-deductible plans guarantee you a great return on your money.

To set up an IRA account, you may contact several different places, such as your bank, brokerage, financial institution, or insurance company. It is important to know that most of these institutions are FDIC insured. Be sure and check that the place where you invest your money is insured by the FDIC.

SEP IRA

Self-employee pensions, created for the self-employed, allow employer contributions as well. In 2003, you are allowed to put a total of $40,000, or a total of 25 percent of your income, whichever is less, in the plan. This entire amount is tax-free.

With WWE, I am considered contract labor even though I am contracted exclusively to them. The SEP is what I use for my retirement planning.

When I first came to WWE in December 1995, our contracts were vastly different. The contract was only guaranteeing ten shows a year at $150 a show.

Basically it was a handshake deal. This is the contract I first signed.

I had been in Europe off and on for two years when Bruce Prichard called and said they wanted to talk to me about a tryout. On my way home from Germany, I stopped off in Philadelphia for my tryout. It was snowing very heavily, and they were doing a Pay-Per-View that day.

I was sitting in the back when Tony Garea came up and asked who I was. I told him I was there for a tryout, and he threw me out of the locker room.

I thought, "Great."

So I headed to the airport, but because of the snow I couldn't get a flight home.

Since I couldn't go home, I decided to show up at the arena the next day. This time, in Bethlehem, I got my tryout.

I wrestled Savio Vega. Savio is a great wrestler, and he worked extremely hard for me. Gerry Brisco and J. J. Dillon met me as I returned from the ring. Gerry told me they wanted to sign me and asked if I was going to WCW, the WWE's competition at the time. I told them that if WWE wanted me, then I wouldn't go to

At Universal Studios: Bruce Prichard, Pat Patterson, Bubba Ray Dudley, and Gerry Brisco, who plans to retire to Texas sometime in the future.

the WCW. Gerry told me I had his word, and I told him he had mine. I could sense that Gerry was the type that wouldn't lie. He didn't.

Vince McMahon explained to me in my first meeting that no contract is worth anything but the handshake behind it. He went on to say that his word was good. That was all I needed to know, and we have gotten along ever since.

However, when I signed with WWE, I was supposed to go down and talk to WCW. They had already told me they would give me $75,000 the first year, and the second year was negotiable. I had decided that if WWE wanted me, then I wouldn't go to Atlanta to talk to the WCW.

My father, a lifelong banker, knew that I was going to one place or the other. So when I returned home, he asked where I had agreed to go. I told him WWE. He asked what I was guaranteed, and I told him ten shows at $1,500 a year, but that the contract was just a formality. He asked what WCW wanted to give me. I told him $75,000 to start.

I think he thought he had raised a moron.

It turns out, though, that my inclination was right. I could not have made a better choice.

401(k)s Easily Understood

There are about 30 million Americans involved in a company-sponsored plan such as a 401(k). If you work for a nonprofit organization, then you probably have a very similar tax-deferred savings (retirement) plan, such as a 403(b). Public employees usually have a plan called the 457 plan.

All of these plans are named after their sections in the federal tax code. For example, section 401, subsection k, would be the 401(k). These federal tax guys know their numbers, but they are not so great at creative naming.

All three of these plans basically work the same way. You can put money into them now that will not be taxed and let it grow tax-free using the miracle of compounding interest. You get an instant tax break on the money (because you are putting this money in before taxes), which means that if you are in the

30 percent tax bracket, you get an automatic 30 percent return on your money. This is a great return, and a great incentive to save toward your retirement.

With all of the uncertainty surrounding Social Security these days, it is very foolish not to make provisions for extra income during retirement. I am sure that you have heard how insolvent Social Security is becoming. Whether you believe the direst reports or even the best estimates, then you know odds are that you will receive less than your full share of benefits.

The good thing about the 401(k) plans is that the money in these plans goes in tax-free and won't be taken out until you retire, when it will most likely be in a lower tax bracket. These government-sponsored plans are a win-win situation.

The 401(k) was created by Congress because it came to the realization that Americans were rapidly becoming some of the worst savers in the world. Americans are terrific spenders, which has helped to drive the economy, but they lag behind the rest of the world in savings rates per income. Because of this, Congress created company-sponsored 401(k) programs and gave the participants tax breaks if they would join in these plans.

In 2003, you are able to put $12,000 tax-free into a 401(k) plan. This amount goes up $1,000 every year until 2006. If you are over fifty, you are allowed an extra $1,000 in 2003 and that amount goes up every year by $2,000.

401(k) Contribution Amounts

		Over Fifty
2003	$12,000	$14,000
2004	$13,000	$16,000
2005	$14,000	$18,000
2006	$15,000	$20,000

Most companies agree to match a certain percentage of the money you put into these plans, ranging from 10 to 50 cents on each dollar you contribute.

Very simply put, if your company matches any of your money

in a 401(k), and you do not take advantage of that *free* money, then you are dumb—that is, stupid, or rather ignorant.

This is *free* money; take advantage of this *free* money.

Also, you get a tax deduction for the money you contribute. You are putting this money in before taxes; the government is trying to force you to save. You will not be taxed on this money. This is the equivalent of getting an automatic 30 percent return on your money. This is too good to pass up. Please, if you don't get anything else from this book—other than me being a good guy—be certain you take advantage of all your retirement opportunities.

A 401(k) is something you should max out every year. This is your retirement future.

On average, there are eight to thirteen different funds in the typical 401(k). You will be able to direct your money into the type of portfolio diversification that is best for you, both for your personal risk tolerance and your age in proximity to retirement. We will discuss portfolio diversification in our next chapter. You are able in most of the plans to tailor this amount each year to fit your retirement's needs.

Summary

- **Take off the hubcap—see how compounding interest works for you.**

- **If you see Dutch Mantel or Tom Prichard in a pit crew, bet against the driver.**

- **Always boil plastic-coated wieners; they'll taste better.**

- **Always max out your 401(k). This is your retirement future.**

CHAPTER | 6

LOANER OR OWNER?

Know What Your Money Is Doing

Coins, football cards (except mine), Layfield fishing lures, Beanie Babies, emus, and dinosaur eggs are not where you want to put your hard-earned savings, if you want a return on your money.

If you are just saving these things for personal reasons (then might I suggest my wrestling doll and T-shirts also?), that is fine, but if you are investing for your future, then you have to look to the equity markets.

I can tell you what not to invest in: Tim White's Christmas liquor basket.

Tim White is one of my very good friends, a referee in WWE, and owner of the world-famous Friendly Tap in Comberland, Rhode Island. The Friendly Tap has been used on our TV show, and is just the perfect pub when you think about pubs.

Tim is an exceptionally good person. The problem comes every year at Christmas, when he sells raffle tickets for the liquor basket. Now, Timmy claims that the liquor basket is legit, and so does Tim's friend Arnold Skaaland (one of our Hall of Fame wrestlers). The reason we doubt the validity of Tim and Arnie's claims is because Arnie wins the liquor basket every year, or at least so it seems.

However, every year at Christmas we all buy tickets. Arnie wins, and Tim and Arnie drink for free. You might ask why we continue buying tickets. It is because Tim and Arnie get upset if we don't. It is like our annual charitable contribution.

If you like investing in things like Beanie Babies and Tim and Arnie drinking at Christmas, then you should. However, if you want to invest for your future, then you must look for other options.

Stocks and Bonds

There are two main avenues for investing in the financial world—stocks and bonds. There are many different ways to invest in both of these investment vehicles.

You have to decide whether you want to be a loaner or an owner. If you are investing your money, you are one or the other.

Investing in a company's stocks is actually buying a percentage of the company.

This is being an owner. The number of shares you buy is the part of the company that you own. Owning stock makes you a shareholder in that company, maybe in a small way compared to some, but a shareholder nonetheless. This is how you must look at investing in stocks. This is why it is important to buy stock in companies you *want* to own, not just because the stock price is low. (Buying stock at a low price is just one criterion in purchasing stocks.)

A Loaner

Buying certificates of deposits (CDs), treasury bills, or bonds is being a loaner.

You are loaning money to something or someone that guarantees you a set return on your money. Buying a CD at a bank is loaning money to that bank. Buying bonds in a company is loaning money to that company. The company agrees to return your money with a certain percentage gain, or rate of return.

Purchasing treasury bills is loaning money to the government. The government, in return, will guarantee you a certain percentage gain on your money as thanks for loaning it money. In the same way that war bonds were a way to loan money to the government for the war effort, treasuries are a way of loaning money to the government to ensure a certain return. Unfortunately, you cannot ensure that the government will spend the money wisely.

Being a loaner (buying fixed-income things such as bonds, certificates of deposit, or treasury bills) can be a good way to invest. Almost every well-diversified portfolio has a certain allocation of money that is in some type of fixed-income investment. The closer you get to retirement, the more of a loaner you will be, because it is more of a fixed and dependable income stream.

You must remember the time frame in which you will be investing to establish your personal portfolio diversification. Also you need to know your personal risk tolerance, which no chart in the world can tell you. If you are investing long-term for your retirement, then stocks must be the way to go, at least as a major portion of your portfolio. We will get into portfolio diversification soon.

An Owner

Stocks over the course of Wall Street's history have returned an average of around 11 percent annually. Bonds have returned about half that. But you must look further to understand real return for both stocks and bonds.

Bonds have returned under 6 percent over the same period that stocks have returned 11 percent. The problem with bonds is that they mature at different stages. Because of the different maturity dates, you cannot use the tax haven of long-term capital gains to your advantage.

Capital gains tax means simply that if you hold equities (stocks) for more than a year, then the maximum tax rate you will pay is 20 percent, a rate that some in Congress are trying to lower. You do not pay your normal tax rate, whatever it may be, but only the 20 percent that is referred to as capital gains, because you have met the requirements of the capital gains by holding these equities (stocks) for more than a year.

You do not have such a tax haven with bonds. You will have to pay whatever your normal tax rate is—which could be as high as 35 percent. So you make half the profit on the money you invested in bonds rather than stocks (11 percent for the stocks versus the 6 percent for bonds) and could pay up to almost twice the tax rate.

This is why I believe stocks are far superior to bonds as a long-term investment. I don't believe that bonds are a bad investment—they certainly have their place in a portfolio—I just believe that stocks are by far the superior choice. I believe that history has proven that as fact.

Portfolio Diversification

Diversification is very important to any portfolio. Diversification eliminates a lot of market fluctuations, because normally when the equities market is going well, the bond market is not doing well, and the converse is generally true. When the bond market is doing well, it is usually because the stock market is flagging, forcing people to take their money out of equities and put them into bonds (what the analysts call a "flight to quality"). Having a good complement of stocks and bonds helps assure yourself that you won't lose money in any market—at least, not as much money as you might if you weren't diversified.

One of the great lessons of the 1990s bull market (a market that is going upward is referred to as a bull market, and a market that is going downward is referred to as a bear market) is that there is potential to lose money in the market, especially with speculative stock picking. Those that invested in the dot-com companies that had no earnings, only potential, learned the hard way. Investors during this time were not picking stocks rationally. Remember, you must buy stocks in companies you want to own.

Don't Lose Money

The first rule of investing is to not lose money.

I am not talking about being ultraconservative; I am just saying, be smart. You worked hard to earn this money; don't lose it through foolish investing.

I don't write that to scare you. Investors in the late 1990s chased momentum on certain stocks. The people that lost money lost that money because they didn't pay any attention to fundamentals of the companies in which they were investing. I'll explain these fundamentals later in more detail, but basically, they are the company balance sheets. People were investing in companies they knew nothing about, but thought that their stock price would rise. This is the absolute worst way to make investment decisions.

Bulls, Bears, and Jackasses

On a side note, people that are "bullish" are people that believe the market will move higher. When the market is up, you often hear a market analyst on television say that "the bulls were out in force." This means that the market was full of optimism and moved higher.

Bearish people are ones that believe the market is going lower. People who invest in stocks don't like bears.

Once again animals plague me. I have wrestled a bear, but that bear wasn't bad on my portfolio (I didn't even have one then). It sure hurt my ego, though. Just like the analysts, I don't like bears either.

Jackass isn't a term used on Wall Street; it is used exclusively for my old athletic director. Now I think we have all the animal terms taken care of.

Stocks for the Long Term

Stocks have the greatest long-term level of return of any investment there is; however, they also have much greater volatility. You almost always face greater rewards when you have greater risk. You just have to decide if the risk-reward ratio is worth it to you.

There is always going to be that certain group of people who feel that the greatest risk they can take is burying their money in a mayonnaise jar in the backyard. If you are this type, please quit reading this book and either go see a psychiatrist or move out of the country, but please don't move near me.

The key to good long-term returns is to be invested in the stock market, and if you are invested long-term, the volatility smoothes out nicely.

It is important to understand that there have been many earth-shaking events in the last century, and through it all the stock market has returned an average of 11 percent annually. There were two world wars, the Great Depression, the Korean and Vietnam conflicts, the cold war, Desert Storm, several recessions, the civil rights movement, Y2K, the tragedy on September 11, and Sweetwater winning the 1985 Class AAAA Texas high school state play-off championship. Through all of this the market has returned an average of 11 percent annually. There have been ups and downs, but that is why you invest for the long-term.

Through all of these things in the last century, America has shown that it will continue to grow economically. America has proven that it will continue to be the economic leader and that its good companies will continue to make money.

There are many different ways to be invested in the stock market. While every single way you invest in it, you end up owning stock, there are several ways of going about it.

Mutual Funds

One of the greatest ways to be invested in the stock market is to buy into mutual funds that have a proven track record. Finding a mutual fund's track record is an easy thing to do. *Barron's,* a weekly financial newspaper, is a great source that is chock full of useful information. There are many ways to learn about mutual fund performance on the Internet, also. Finance.Yahoo.com is a superlative Web site that includes information about mutual funds.

For the average investor, a good diversified mutual fund is one of the absolute best investments you can make (the other being index funds). Many people are very busy in life and don't enjoy researching individual stocks. For these people, mutual funds are the ideal investment. Many people out there will become quite wealthy by investing in a good mutual fund and leaving it alone.

One great thing about being invested in stocks is that your investment gains are basically passive income. You don't have to actively work to make the money. You don't have to put on a suit, go to the office, and put up with people all day to earn money in the stock market. You do need to do a little research, but your earnings are still considered passive income.

The main thing is to find a mutual fund that has produced better-than-average results for the last five to ten years. Once you find a fund you are interested in, then there are several ways to look up its performance, especially over the Internet. Finance.Yahoo.com and *Barron's* are easy ways to look up mutual fund performance.

Mutual funds are one of the investment vehicles that you cannot withdraw money from on a whim. This is good. It is important to invest in something you cannot get your money out of very easily. I know a lot of people who try to save money, but are never able to because they always have something come up on which they can justify spending their savings. Believe me, something will always come up for which you will need extra money. It is important to realize that if you take $5,000 out of your retirement savings, then you are losing a great deal of money. You may think it is $5,000 you are spending for something—an air-conditioner problem, a new car down payment, or five hundred Bradshaw T-shirts—but when you realize you have taken money out of its compounding interest state, you are losing a great deal more.

That $5,000 after twenty-eight years with an average 11 percent return would be worth $80,000. Now that is an expensive air conditioner.

It is very important to consider money that you have saved for your future as money that is gone or money you have spent. However you need to think of it, it is money that you cannot touch. When you spend your retirement money, you are spending your future away.

So where do you get the money for your air conditioner or other expenditure? Where would you get it if you didn't have money in the bank? You will find a way, just as you always have, to pay off certain things. Try to never touch your retirement account until you need it for retirement.

A mutual fund is a collection of stocks managed by a professional. This gives you an opportunity to buy into this collection of stocks without having to individually own all of the stocks. A good mutual fund is something you can invest your money in regularly in equal amounts, and not have to worry about researching the fund every time. Just occasionally check on it.

Another Gratuitous Shot at My Old Athletic Director

Owning a mutual fund is like owning part of the NFL. You know the whole league is going to make money. You don't know that every team is. You could buy an individual team that is successful, and odds are, their success will continue. However, all kinds of things could possibly come up. Your quarterback could get hurt, or free agency could affect your team—or, even worse, your old athletic director could be named general manager of the team in which you invested. Now that would be disastrous.

It would be much safer to invest your money in the whole NFL if you could; mutual funds allow you to do this. Volatility is reduced because you own a part of a greater number of stocks.

By the way, if you do buy the NFL, would you make me eligible for my pension?

A mutual fund may include fifty stocks. When you buy into that fund, you get a portion of all fifty companies that the mutual owns stock in. Every company in that portfolio may not have a good return, which is why you have many companies in a fund. On average, you will receive a good return.

Types of Mutual Funds

There are many different classifications of funds from which to choose. Big-cap (capitalization) funds invest only in companies with a certain market capitalization, usually around $8 billion and up. Market capitalization is the amount the company is worth in the market.

Mid-cap funds would invest in companies that are in a certain capitalization between small and large. Pretty complex, huh?

Every fund has certain criteria that it has assigned to itself so that the individual will know what kind of companies he or she is buying into.

There are also foreign funds, designated to a certain foreign field or country. There are also bond funds that deal with fixed income investments.

There is virtually every type of fund imaginable. There are even socially conscious funds that won't invest in tobacco or alcohol products. I don't think there is a sinner fund—one that invests in strip bars, alcohol, and legal prostitution—but you never know.

There are also funds within certain criteria that are designated growth funds. So while they might be big-cap funds, they also have to meet certain other requirements, such as growing at a certain rate over the past number of years. You might ask, Why wouldn't everyone invest in companies that grow fast? Many do. The people who don't know that companies are growing faster than the markets. We will talk about company pricing later.

Beginning in Mutual Funds

Starting off in mutual funds is easy. I would start off with a good well-proven domestic growth mutual fund or a domestic big-cap fund. These are funds that are made up of high-growth companies or big capitalization companies in the United States. There are over 10,000 companies in the United States with common stock. With so many great U.S. companies, there is not much need, initially, to look overseas.

When you start investing in overseas companies, you also have to deal with local currency issues and political problems that could arise. It is much easier to invest in U.S. companies. However, after you have gotten started investing, you will need to branch out into international stocks to balance your portfolio, but they will never make up a huge percentage of your portfolio. Keep it around 10 percent.

There will come a time when you will need to diversify your portfolio even with your mutual funds; however, you still don't need to own a great number of funds. Just own good funds. There are way too many funds out there to even consider owning one that has a history of subpar returns.

I believe owning about five mutual funds would be a good number. You want to own a fund that concentrates on big-cap companies in the United States, one that buys overseas stocks such as in the Euro-Pacific region, one small-cap stock fund, one income-building fund, and perhaps another growth or a mid-cap fund. That should be enough diversification.

Every year one fund or another has a phenomenal return. This fund gets the media attention, and the fund manager gets all kinds of praise and honors. After all of this attention is heaped onto this fund and manager, then money flow will follow. This is the amount of money that new investors are pouring into the fund. A track record is not made in one to three years, however.

It takes years to establish a record worthy of notice. This is where you want to invest your money. Anybody can have a great return one year, but consistency over time is much harder to attain. While the past cannot always predict the future, it can be a pretty good indicator.

Momentum Chasing

In the stock market, it is usually not a good idea to follow momentum. In other words, when a stock or fund has a great performance, a lot of people and a lot of money usually follow. This surge in demand drives the stock prices up further. This is chasing momentum.

Chasing momentum is a bad way to buy anything. If you want to buy an old truck, and you know it is worth $5,000, then you would like to purchase it for $5,000 or less. If a couple of other people start bidding on the truck, they will drive the price of the truck higher, perhaps over the $5,000 it is worth. The truck is still just worth $5,000, but it will cost you more than it is worth to buy it. This is an example of how momentum can take prices out of line.

Remember: *Don't try to time the market. Time in the market is more important.*

You can buy from one fund family, such as American Funds, which has all of these funds under its umbrella—or you can mix and choose. However, make sure that these funds have proven records and that the management that produced these returns is still intact.

Normally, there is no reason to sell a mutual fund. Hold on to them forever. I only am writing about these things to let you know that there is a chance that things can change within a fund. Changes demand that you inspect the funds. *This is your money. Take care of it.* A mutual fund posting losses one year is not necessarily a reason to sell that fund. There will be losses. The key is to observe what is happening long-term.

Never chase the newest, hottest fund. This is a basic rule. Find a good fund and stay with it; just be aware that things could change.

You Can Only See as Far as Your Headlights Allow

Things change in business, as they do everywhere. When you are driving a car at night, you can only see as far as your headlights allow you to see. Whatever trouble is past those headlights or whatever good roads are past those headlights, you cannot see. You have to stay alert so you can see the potential trouble as far in advance as possible, as soon as it comes into view.

This is the best way to invest. You can only see as far as your headlights allow you to see. You also can only invest confidently as far as the foreseeable future. This isn't written to alarm you; I am writing this to let you know that while you invest in good companies now, you still must stay vigilant with your investments. Things can change. Even if a fund has a history of good returns, you still need to remain watchful, because things can always change.

Do Two Superbowls Equal a Dynasty?

After the Dallas Cowboys' first of two consecutive Super Bowl victories in the 1990s, you would think that everything was going great internally. You would have every reason to believe that a dynasty was born, and if you lived near Dallas, you would love it. Very few people would believe that just a year later Jerry Jones and Jimmy Johnson would develop irreconcilable differences, and Jimmy would leave.

Sometimes there is trouble just beyond the headlights that you cannot see, and no possible way to see it.

This happens in the corporate world as well. That is why you have to stay up on your investments. Investing long-term is the best way to invest, but do not be blind. Sometimes a little pruning of your investments is necessary, because the climate you first invested in has changed. Normally, a little pruning will be all that you need, not wholesale changes.

Even the great Warren Buffett, recognized as the greatest investor of all time, prunes his portfolio occasionally. Mr. Buffett is one of the great believers of long-term investing, but he knows he still has to remain alert to changes in the businesses in which he invests.

My advice is to buy and hold, *not* buy and ignore.

When Financial Advisers Are Helpful

This is where a good financial planner can come in handy. I believe that you can invest on your own. I believe that you can make decisions on your own. But I also know that it can never hurt to get advice from a person that makes a living giving advice.

One of the purposes of this book is not just to help you understand the market, but also to let you know that when you choose an adviser, you must understand what he is doing with your money. You must know what you want done with it.

If you are just starting investing and have less than $25,000, I would not recommend getting a financial adviser. I would recommend you simply buy into a good proven mutual fund or an index fund, such as the S&P 500 index or the Wilshire 5000 index fund.

Once you get over $25,000 and are getting closer to $50,000, you should consider talking to a financial adviser. It never hurts to seek advice from a person who makes their living doing what you are trying to do. I left a $25,000 gap as to when you should seek help. If you feel it is necessary, seek advice. Everybody is different. If you don't plan to ever look at your retirement portfolio, then I definitely advise seeking help sooner.

You need to count the amount you have in your company retirement plan, because this is part of your overall portfolio.

It is important, if and when you choose to go to an adviser, to tell her your goals, dreams, and what you desire for your future. Going to an adviser with a lump sum of money and asking for help without her knowing anything about you or your financial situation is akin to going to a doctor and asking him to write you a prescription without his ever examining you or asking any questions. A doctor has to have as much information as possible to treat you in the best way. So does a financial adviser.

A good financial adviser or planner is a great thing to have. Good financial adviser can steer you in the right direction long-term. They are much like weathermen. If you ask a weatherman (or weatherwoman) if it will rain next Tuesday, he can give you an educated guess that could turn out right.

If you ask a weatherman if it will be hot in July and August, he will almost certainly be right. He can only see as far as the head-lights go. He can guess what is past those headlights and be quite accurate. An educated guess is still a guess, but overall trends of the market can be predicted fairly successfully.

Ginseng, Loose Bowels, Seoul, and a Pretty Woman Yelling "Rape!"

I learned a valuable lesson in Seoul several years ago about how the future can be easy to predict. I was buying leather jackets in the Itaewon shopping district when the store owner brought me a drink of ginseng. I had never had straight ginseng before. I will never have it again.

I drank the ginseng and almost immediately realized that I had an urgent call to go to the bathroom. In fact, very urgent. I asked the store owner if he had a bathroom. He told me that the closest bathroom was in Wendy's, a couple of blocks away. So with my rear end squeezed as tight as possible, I took off running. I got to Wendy's, ran upstairs to the bathroom, and opened the door.

The bathroom was a unisex bathroom with two stalls, one for men and one for women, with a vanity separating them. I checked the men's door and found it to be locked. I looked under the stall and saw two feet. I was now seconds away from being as embarrassed as I ever could be.

I knocked on the door, and there was no answer. I knocked again. I finally heard the toilet flush. I realized I just might make it. I unbuttoned my jeans and started to unzip my fly, realizing I was down to seconds to being utterly humiliated. I needed to be ready when the door opened. I was down to seconds.

Then something totally shocking happened. A very good-looking blond woman walked out of the men's stall. She did not know she was in a unisex bathroom and that she was in the men's stall. All she knew was that she was in a women's bathroom (so she thought), and here was a large man waiting on her with his pants unbuckled.

She screamed.

Correct that. She screamed loudly.

I tried to explain, but she just kept screaming. The problem was, I still had to go, and soon. So I rushed past her into the stall and gratefully did my business.

However, there was still a woman outside screaming.

By the time I came out, the police were there also. Fortunately, they understood the situation and tried to explain it to the lady. She was not interested in listening. She just wanted to keep calling me names like pervert and other things similar to what Bruce Prichard called me.

I saw the lady from the rest room many times the rest of the week at the Itaewon shopping district. She usually pointed me out to her group, and they would cross the street.

I felt like an ex-con.

Now you would think a person with any planning ability would be able to know that something like this could happen in an American restaurant chain with a unisex bathroom. That lady should be mad at the building designer, not me.

A good planner or adviser can generally be right long-term about the market. But if you ask him if a certain stock will go up by next week, he can only give you an educated guess, just as a meteorologist would give you an educated guess about the weather that will happen on a certain day next week. Long-term trends are more easily spotted than what will happen by next month.

While I do recommend a financial adviser, I don't recommend giving your money to someone and letting him put it wherever he wants to. He should explain to you every time what he is going to do, and ask your permission to invest. *He works for you.* It is your money. *Know* what your money is doing.

A good adviser will gladly take time to let you know what he thinks your money should be invested in.

If he doesn't, take three steps back, pick up this book, and hit him between the eyes. Wipe up the blood, tell him "thank you," and go somewhere else.

Listening with a Discerning Ear

One of the great forms of information today is financial news networks such as CNBC, which I feel is the best source of market news on television. The regular hosts and commentators on their shows are the best on television. One would pay a lot of money for the information dispersed daily by guys like Joe Kernen, David Faber, Mark Haines, Bill Griffith, and others. These guys have access to CEOs and the movers and shakers on Wall Street. They collect and present this information daily to their viewers. Watching these and other financial shows is a good way of keeping up with what the market feels is important.

One of the problems with these shows is the guest analysts that regularly appear on them. It is not that these analysts say or do anything wrong; most of them are some of the best professional money managers in the business today. The problem is, they talk about very current events and how that will affect the market, perhaps in as short a time frame as today or tomorrow. This tends to involve speculation, although very educated speculation. I don't want to invest my money on speculation.

Television has become as results-oriented as the rest of the world. When these analysts who are so knowledgeable are on these shows, they are often put at a disadvantage. They are asked what is going to happen to the market this week or this month, which is almost impossible to predict. If they were to be asked about how companies will perform for the next ten years, then you would see their expertise. Long-term stock picking is an easy thing to do; short-term involves a lot of guessing and momentum chasing.

The key is to listen with a discerning ear to what these guys are saying about how the companies will be affected long-term, not just next week or next month. Most of these guys are very knowledgeable about the market and the companies they cover. Most analysts are assigned certain sectors of the market, and that is where they spend their time and effort.

The problem that these analysts face, and the problem that some of the reporters face, is that the viewing audience wants to know what is going to happen now, and this goes back to the weatherman analogy. Long term is easy to predict; short term is a guess.

A good financial planner, just like these guys, can guess about what will happen next week, but he can with much more certainty tell you what will happen for the next five years or more.

Remember, a lot of people out there would enjoy separating you from your money, so be careful. It is best to go to a pro that comes from a nationwide, reputable company. It is important to remember that he works for you, and if at any point you feel he is not the one for you, leave. You would be surprised how many people won't do this. *This is your money.* Don't let yourself be taken for a ride with it.

My First and Only Financial Adviser

The first professional I went to was an Edward Jones representative in my hometown, Dan Weber. I was immediately impressed with his knowledge, but I also knew that he could just be a used car salesman. History has shown that he was one of the best things that could've happened to me. Dan, like most professionals should do, took time to educate me on everything he was doing with my money. A good professional will never keep what he is doing from you, but rather will go to lengths to explain it to you. A good pro should be doing research himself, not just taking the companies' recommendations.

My mentor and friend, Dan Weber. Dan's in the front.

Of course, the fact that Dan drives a Harley and shoots a very good game of pool impressed me also. Maybe that was his way of relating to his clients, or maybe he just had a misspent youth. Either way, he is great with his knowledge of the markets and asset allocation, and he is also a good friend. Dan has been a good mentor to me.

A good financial adviser will be a mentor to you. He or she should explain everything to you so that you will know and understand what your money is doing. More importantly, you can make your own choices about where you want your money invested.

A good financial adviser is one that will eventually wean you from him. You will only need a routine checkup with him instead of a complete overhaul that you don't understand. It is a power trip for some advisers to keep you in the dark about where your money is invested. This way you will always have to rely on them. Also, there are no checks and balances on these guys if you don't understand what they are doing.

It is your money—ask questions. If you don't get the answers you want, leave. Just as there are good doctors and bad doctors, yet they have all graduated from medical school, there are good financial planners and bad financial planners. Don't be fooled by certificates on the wall, or letters behind their names. Most of these guys are certainly well trained, but that doesn't make them good. I have seen rotten mechanics that are old and have been working on cars for a long time. Doing something a long time doesn't necessarily make you good at it, nor does being trained. Carl Lewis, Jesse Owens, and Michael Johnson could train me to run a hundred-yard dash for the next twenty years, yet I will never be any good at it, because I am just too slow. You can't make a silk purse out of a sow's ear.

Sweetwater vs. Abilene High

My high school football team was playing against one of our rivals, Abilene High School, my junior year. Abilene High had a middle linebacker that was, I think, about thirty years old and weighed about three hundred pounds. Now understand, my high school had a great football program, and we did beat Abilene that year. But this linebacker, who looked like he was older than most of our coaches, was wreaking havoc on our offense and our running backs, who were really wishing we would block him. And we did beat Abilene High that year.

Coach W. T. Stapler asked me at halftime if I could get to him on a trap play. I replied that I was sure that I could get to him, but I was also sure it wouldn't do any good. It turned out I was right, I *could* get to him—but it didn't do any good. You see, all the training in the world still boils down to being able to apply it. And the only one getting executed that night on that stinking trap play was *me*. However, we did beat Abilene High that year.

Did I mention that we beat Abilene High that year? We did.

Just because a person is trained and knows what to do does not mean they are able to do it. Don't be fooled by degrees on a wall or big words by an adviser. This is your money. Judge the adviser for yourself. Talk to other people who have used him.

Good advisers take a little looking to find, but they are definitely worth the hunt.

Index Funds

Another great way to invest in the stock market and limit your risk is an index fund, a compilation of a certain group of stocks. There are all kinds of index funds available. Most 401(k) retirement funds have at least the S&P index fund available, which is a great fund. The S&P is the benchmark a lot of mutual funds compare themselves to every year. I have always figured, why buy a comparison when you can buy the benchmark? The Wilshire 5000 is another index fund that mirrors the entire market.

Index funds are a fantastic way to invest in the stock market. There are all kinds of index funds. The NASDAQ 100 is one of the most popular indices. The NASDAQ 100 consists of the hundred biggest capitalization stocks in the NASDAQ, minus any financial companies. It is built to be mainly a technology index. It is a way of investing in a wide range of technology stocks while limiting your risks because you are diversified.

It is an important thing to note exactly what companies compose your index. For instance, the triple Qs are made up primarily of the four biggest companies in the NASDAQ. If you own a large-cap mutual or aggressive growth fund, odds are you already own these companies in some quantity. It is important to know what you own; this is your money that you have worked very hard to earn. Take the time to consider the makeup of your mutual funds, plus the makeup of the index funds you have purchased or are considering purchasing.

You can buy index funds in virtually anything today—pharmaceutical index, semiconductor index. Index funds are one of the best ways to diversify in today's market. You can choose to buy a whole index of one type of stocks and not have to worry about individual failures. I once read an article that said diversification is for people who aren't willing to do their own research and be diligent about it. The problem with this basic assumption is that most people have lives and jobs, and can't spend all day watching and researching the market. Neither should they have to. Buying these index funds takes a lot of the guesswork out of investing. The first time I went to buy my own furniture, I learned a very important lesson. Cindy and I had been out of the trailer for a couple of years now, and it looked like I was going to stay employed by the McMahon family, the owners of WWE, for a while. However, once you are poor, you understand that you could be that way again, and you are hesitant to buy anything over two dollars. Most of our furniture—okay, all of our furniture—was from the Just Married period, which was just after the Victorian period, and it wasn't very nice. Actually, it would have to have been better to have been not very nice.

Owen Hart and a House Full of Furniture

The story actually started a few weeks earlier when unfortunately I had to attend a funeral of a very good friend, Owen Hart. Owen had died in a tragic accident in Kansas City in Kemper Arena. He died while doing a stunt that he had practiced several times. Somehow the stunt went horribly and tragically, fatally wrong while he was performing it in front of the live audience. We actually wrestled a couple of matches after this happened.

I felt so sorry for Vince McMahon that night; you could just see that his heart was breaking with the decision of what to do. Either way he went, people were going to say that he was wrong. If the show continued, they would say that he was callous and uncaring. If the show were canceled, they would say he should have continued, to keep the people's minds off the tragedy. There was no right answer. Personally, I would have done the same thing he did. I am just glad I didn't have to make that decision.

Vince flew everybody that wanted to attend to Owen Hart's funeral. He paid, literally, for everything. I have always admired him for that. Vince and his family, for everything that the media says negatively about him, is a first-class guy. I believe that it is just that Vince is not a puppet for the media, and for this they do not like him, sometimes.

As I was sitting at Owen's funeral and listening to his beautiful wife give such a lovely eulogy and talk about the fact that they were just about to move into their dream house, it broke my heart. The world lost a good man when it lost Owen.

Owen had won two Slammy awards while he was wrestling and had given one to Collin Raye's son Jake. Owen really liked Collin's son, even calling him on all of his birthdays. Collin (one of the great country-and-western singers of our time) really felt a deep appreciation of Owen for the way that Owen cared for Jake. With tears in his eyes, Collin sang the prettiest rendition of "Amazing Grace" at Owen's funeral I had ever heard. It was one of those moments in life that you know at the time that you will never forget. This was a tribute worthy of Owen.

I called Cindy from the airport, and she was crying. She explained to me that Owen and I were about the same age, and we had both worked for Otto and Peter in Europe. It could have just as easily have been me that died, she said. With all that had just happened on my mind, I told her that we had held off so long on buying furniture and redoing our house, we should go ahead and do what we planned. I think this eased her mourning.

This was a great decision I made. There is nothing I love more in this world than my wife, and the pride she has in our home makes me very happy. She actually is not a spendthrift—it just makes for a better story to blame the furniture expenses on her. I certainly can't blame anything on me, I'm a man.

As we were shopping for furniture in Tyler, Texas, just thirty-five miles from my hometown of Athens, Texas, I was amazed at the responses I was getting from the furniture salesmen. All of them were comparing their furniture to the local Ethan Allen furniture store. I finally decide that if Ethan Allen was so superlative that the other salesmen had to compare their furniture to them, then maybe I should visit that store. I have been very happy ever since.

Buying stocks, whether through index funds, mutual funds, or individual stocks, is much the same as buying that furniture from Ethan Allen. Why would you spend your hard-earned money on less quality when you have a choice? With more than 10,000 companies from which to choose, there is no reason not to invest in the best the market has to offer.

Angela Dietrich and Cindy. Angela—a good friend—is the salesperson for Ethan Allen; she has cost me a lot of money.

I think index funds are the same way. Every fund manager compares themselves to a certain index. My question would be, Why not just buy the index? Makes sense to me. If something is that good, then why not just buy it? I believe the answer is simply human nature. Everyone wants the long shot—the fund that beats the index. But don't get me wrong; there *are* funds that beat the indices.

Buying an index is boring, making money is not. I would prefer to be bored and make money.

Portfolio Diversification

When I talk of your portfolio, I am talking about your retirement portfolio made up of stocks, bonds, and cash. I am not talking about your total net worth, such as your house or your belongings. I am also not talking about real estate or other investments you have.

It is important to remember that you have to consider your entire portfolio, not just one section. For instance, if you have your 401(k) and an on-line trading account, you need to include all of this together in your portfolio.

Portfolio diversification is what ties all these things together. There will be only three things in your portfolio: loaner, owner, and cash. Everything works from these three things.

First, you will have equities (stocks), which is being an owner. You will own stocks through mutual funds, individual stocks, and index funds.

Second, you will be a loaner, which includes bonds, bond funds, CDs, and treasuries.

Third, you will have cash. Do I have to explain? That is your money market or savings account. However, it is not your day-to-day cash money; it is your retirement cash money.

The whole key is how you diversify this money. This will differ according to age and how close you are to retirement. Actually, how close you are to retirement is much more important.

Portfolio diversification is very similar to dating different types of women. You date pretty ones, and you date ugly ones, but on average you are doing okay.

There are many different theories about portfolio diversification and asset allocation. One of these theories is to use age as your guide to determine the stock-bond ratio in your portfolio. For example, if you are twenty-five years old, then you would have 25 percent of your portfolio in bonds and the rest in stocks. Every year you get older, you would add a percent to your bond portion. By the time you are seventy, you would have 70 percent of your portfolio in bonds. Of course, if you live past a hundred, then you have a problem. It is hard to put 102 percent of your portfolio into bonds.

This is a reasonable way to diversify. The older you get, the less fluctuation you want in your portfolio, because you need a steadier stream of income. Actually, it is more your closeness to retirement that determines how much you need in fixed income such as bonds.

While this theory, like most of them, makes sense on the surface, absolutely no theory can determine your personal aversion to risk. If you are the type of person that worries incessantly, then you need to adjust your portfolio to where you won't drive yourself, and your spouse, crazy. However, if you worry that much, you probably aren't married, or you have already driven your spouse crazy anyway. If you bought dried food, generators, water, and unregistered guns to get ready for the year 2000, then there is no portfolio chart in the world that you could go by. You should seek counseling for yourself, not for your money. Simply, you are too goofy to know better.

Life is about living, and your portfolio should give you comfort—not concern. While you can use certain theories about asset allocation as a guide, you have to personalize your portfolio for your own needs and comfort level.

There are times when bonds will do much better than equities and there are times when equities will do much better than bonds. A diverse portfolio allows you to weather these times, and on average, you will do well.

The further you are away from retirement, the more you should have in the equities market. The reason is because stocks return almost twice over time what bonds do, but they are more volatile. When you have time, the volatility is smoothed out. If you have a short time frame, you could be getting in on a downturn (bear market), and you may not have time to weather the storm.

Here is a typical example of portfolio diversification:

Twenty-Plus Years to Retirement

65% stocks

30% bonds

5% cash

Again, remember that these are standard diversifications. Every individual is different. If you are going to sweat every market downturn, you should be more conservative—perhaps 50 percent bonds, and 45 percent stocks. Or make up your own portfolio; you might want more cash. If you have a job that could come to a sudden end or layoffs are prevalent at your company, you will need more cash in case of an emergency.

If you have a long time to retirement, and you feel comfortable with reasonable risk, then you might want more of your portfolio in stocks. This is the way I feel.

The main thing to realize is that this is just a suggestion; it is not set in stone. You must tailor your portfolio to fit your needs and personality. This is your hard-earned money, and your retirement. Spend a little time on it. You spend a lot of time making the money; spend some on where to put it.

Ten Years to Retirement

60% stocks

35% bonds

5% cash

Again tailor your portfolio to fit your needs. Start reducing your equity holdings every year you are closer to retirement.

Five Years to Retirement

60% bonds

30% stocks

10% cash

Most of your retirement plans allow you to adjust your portfolio with no charge. You will have to adjust your portfolio at least annually, because it will get out of balance. For instance, if stocks are having a great year, then by the end of the year you will be too heavy in stocks, because they will have grown out of proportion to the rest of your portfolio.

Adjusting your portfolio annually forces you to sell either stocks or bonds that have had a run-up, thereby locking in your profit. Conversely, it forces you to buy the things that have not done well. Therefore, you are getting them on sale.

If your retirement account does not allow you to adjust without penalty, meaning you have to sell either your stocks or bonds to adjust your portfolio, you will be stuck with a tax bill. You should simply take the new money you are putting in your retirement account every week or month and put it toward the part of your portfolio that needs a bigger percentage. That way you aren't losing profits to Uncle Sam.

Stock Diversification

Within your portfolio, you also must diversify your stock holdings. When I mention stocks as a broad term for your portfolio, it is important to realize that you must diversify them within their allotment of your portfolio as well.

Large company stocks (blue chips) that make a lot of money and have a good balance sheet (they have paid dividends out to stockholders for decades) will make up most of your stock holdings—usually around 40–50 percent. These are your big companies, the proverbial 800-pound gorillas—companies such as GE, Wal-Mart, Microsoft, Dell, McDonald's, Citigroup, Merck, and Gillette. These are your tried-and-true companies that should be around and make a lot of money for a long time.

Mid-cap stocks generally make up between 10–20 percent of the stock part of your portfolio.

Small company stocks will generally make up between 15–30 percent of your stock portfolio. Small company stocks are generally considered companies that have a market capitalization under $800,000,000, like JAKKS Pacific and WWE.

International stocks will make up 15–25 percent of your stock portfolio. International stocks are your companies that are based abroad, such as Vodafone or Fuji Film.

Remember, I am talking here about percentages of stock in your stock portfolio—not as a percentage of your entire portfolio.

Individual stocks are something that we will get into the next two chapters. This is my favorite part.

Summary

- Stocks have produced twice the returns of bonds over the history of the market.

- An index fund and a large-cap mutual fund are the two best investment vehicles when starting out.

- Sweetwater beat Abilene High in football in 1984, while playing in P. E. Shotwell Stadium at Abilene.

- Buy and hold, *don't* buy and ignore.

- Go with your wife to shop for furniture; she cannot be trusted.

- Don't win back-to-back Super Bowls; you could be fired.

- Know what your money is doing. It is your money.

CHAPTER | 7

STOCK PICKING

Choose Your Advisers Carefully

Don't go to a fat doctor and ask for advice on how to lose weight. Choose your advisers carefully. Makes sense, doesn't it? Then why do so many people make such glaring errors in judgment?

I used to hate the salesman that would present this whole great get-rich-quick scheme, explaining how everyone who was doing it was making a ton of money. Yet, when you would see him leave, he would be driving a beat-up old car. I guess everyone was making a ton of money except him.

If you go to a gym and ask for a personal trainer, and your trainer looks more like a cellulite storage facility than Arnold Schwarzenegger, would you stay? Of course not. Then why do so many people take advice in the stock market from people who have had no success themselves? Don't go to fat doctors to ask how to lose weight, and don't go to people who have had no success in the stock market for investment advice.

Helping Foreigners Learn English

Some advice is good. Other advice is not.

When Cindy and I were living in Bremen, Germany, I was helping Hiro Yamamoto, a wrestler from Japan, learn English. Hiro worked for one of the two major wrestling alliances in Japan. His particular alliance was owned by Antonio Anoki, the same wrestler who fought Muhammad Ali. Every year Mr. Anoki would pick one of his promising young wrestlers and send him to

Europe for the seven-month tour to further his wrestling skills. This also would help these young men learn English, because they would be in constant contact with English-speaking people on the tours.

Hiro was a really good guy who was trying to learn English and everything else he could, so several of the other wrestlers and I would help him every way *we* could.

Christmas greetings from Europe: Otto Wanz is on the far right, Peter William on the far left, Dave Finlay in the middle. I am in the back with Tony St. Clair, August Smisl, and Luc Porier.

Otto Wanz, an extremely large man, paid us every other day. Otto was one of Austria's favorite sons. He grew up in Graz, Austria, the home place of Arnold Schwarzenegger. Otto was second only in popularity to the Austrian oak, Arnold. Otto was a great guy to work for and typical of the fun-loving Austrian people.

I explained to Hiro that it is customary to say "Thank you" when receiving money. Wanting Hiro to excel in the social graces, I also taught him the best way to say thank you was to look up at Otto after he received his money and say "Is that it, Fat Man?" I explained that Otto might act surprised, but that his surprise would be astonishment at how good Hiro's English had become. Otto did act very surprised.

Otto also laughed. I really enjoyed being around Otto.

Choose your advisers carefully.

I can help you with your financial success; linguistically you are on your own.

Stock Picking

Stock picking is much more than hunches and hot tips from your second cousin's brother-in-law. My second cousin's brother-in-law, Joel Stukas, is probably not a good stock picker either. However, he did run one of the best restaurants in town, Jam's in Athens, Texas. I guess it would be okay to eat with him, but don't get stock tips from him.

I think he cheats at golf also.

Buy-and-Hold Doesn't Mean Buy-and-Ignore

Long-term investing has proven over time to be superior to short-term investing and day trading. There is a difference between investing, trading, and speculating. Remember, *Long Term, Long Term, and Long Term.*

The thing that I am exposing is long-term investing, which is investing for the *foreseeable* future. I believe that you should own stock or a mutual forever, or until something has fundamentally changed.

Whenever you buy a stock that simply has been beaten down and you believe that it will go up, you are speculating in the stock market. This is how many people lose money. While it is prudent to buy a company's stock when it is discounted, it is not prudent to buy that stock for the sole reason that it has lost a lot of its value. There usually is a good reason that companies lose value.

A good company that you like that loses value can be a bargain, but understand, it is still about fundamentals. Prices in the stock market fluctuate, just as prices fluctuate elsewhere. If a company is sound and nothing has changed, and you see a dip in its stock price, then you are getting a bargain for your money, and it could be the time to buy that stock.

Money is too hard to come by to invest on hunches, not sound decisions. This is your money. You have worked hard for it. Don't blow your money speculating when you can be investing. Investing it correctly makes more sense.

Short-Term Trading

Trading is another thing that is best left up to the professionals. The average individual, who does a little research, can do investing long-term. Trading, or buying stocks for the purpose of selling them in a short time, such as three to six months or less, should be left to those who are pros. I promise you this is a way to lose a lot of money, and believe me, a lot of people have lost a lot of money doing this.

A little knowledge can be a dangerous thing. It is this way with everything you do in life. Travel a little. The more you travel, the more you realize how little you have actually seen.

A little knowledge can get you in trouble. This has happened to a lot of day traders who thought they knew what they were doing. Trading is a speculative thing that takes more than a little knowledge. I would say *luck* is the main prerequisite. Remember, what I advocate is investing, not trading.

Brad Rheingans and His Stupid Tree

I think Brad enjoyed showing a young ex-professional football player what a great wrestler he still was. Every day we would wrestle down on the mat for conditioning; Brad usually volunteered to wrestle with me. So for about three straight months I had humility lessons. Brad also had this stupid tree I would have to pick up and throw around for conditioning. I really hated that tree.

Muhammad Ali said that one of the reasons that he didn't want to go to Vietnam was because the Vietcong had never done anything to him. Well, that tree had never done anything to me. Brad would have us pick up this stupid tree trunk, throw it over our heads, then go get it, pick it back up, and throw it over our heads again. That tree had never done anything to me. I did not want to throw it anywhere.

The tree was about six feet tall and a foot and a half in diameter. It was worn completely smooth by all of the people who had handled it over the years. I would be willing to bet that that tree hadn't done anything to them either.

I don't know what Brad had against trees, but something must have happened to him in his childhood. Maybe he fell out of a tree when he was very young. I do know Brad had serious issues with this tree that should have been dealt with by a professional.

Upon finishing my training with Brad, I came back home to Texas to start wrestling. Because of Brad's well-respected name, I had several opportunities to wrestle. On the second night I was to wrestle, I was booked in the Sportatorium in Dallas, Texas. This was a huge treat for me. All the early wrestling that I watched had been broadcast from this building. Now I was going to get to wrestle there—in the same building and ring that the Von Erichs, Freebirds, and Bruiser Brody had made famous.

This night when I arrived, I learned that Al Perez Jr. had flight problems and couldn't make it to the show. Al was in the main event with Rod Price for the heavyweight championship. Now a replacement was sorely needed. The promoters knew virtually nothing about me except that I was big—and that Brad Rheingans had trained me. They probably also had heard that I could beat up a decent-sized tree. Since several people there knew Brad very well, the promoter decided to take a chance and put me in the main event with Rod.

That same night, as fate would have it, Kendo Nagasaki had come over from Japan to look for new talent for his Japanese promotion. He saw me and knew he had never heard of me, so he asked who I was. They told him that Brad Rheingans had trained me, and I was working in the main event, so he asked me if I wanted to come to Japan in a couple of weeks. I said I would love to. Kendo obviously had never seen me wrestle, or he would not have booked me. The only thing that Kendo knew was that Brad had trained me and I was wrestling in the main event. Kendo figured I must know what I was doing.

He was wrong.

I knew absolutely nothing about wrestling in Japan, but when I told some of the guys I was going there, they could hardly believe it. Certain guys there had spent years wrestling in the Sportatorium and had never been asked to go to Japan. Back then it was quite an honor to go to Japan. I would find out soon why it was hard.

These Guys Are Good. What Am I Doing Here?

Japan in those days was, physically, a hard place to wrestle. A lot of the wrestling was real. What I mean by this is that there were a lot of well-trained wrestlers there who enjoyed beating and tying up young talent. Young talent usually was lunch to these guys. I did not know this.

You have to understand that just because someone is supposed to win a match and the other wrestler agrees to this, a lot of things can still happen from bell to bell. For instance, if one wrestler is supposed to win and the other doesn't like the outcome, then he can go into the ring and literally beat the first guy up and then make it look real dumb and phony that he lost. The "loser" will still let the right guy win; he will just make a point through physicality that he doesn't like it. This is how Japanese wrestling was when I first went over there.

Fixed, Not Fake

I have always said that wrestling is not fake. It is fixed. There is no way that you can say getting hit over the head with a metal chair is fake. It hurts too bad to be fake. Wrestling is fixed, at least most of the time. There are always instances that have happened where someone gets mad, or it was just a planned double-cross. For the most part, though, it is fixed. *Fake* is a word that I don't believe applies.

I had a bar fight scene one day with Val Venis, and he mistakenly hit me in the face with a pool cue. The cue went all the way through my cheek. It took a couple of hours to get the hole in my face sewed up. When I got home, someone asked me if that was supposed to happen. I replied, "Yes, that it was supposed to happen. Val was supposed to put the pool cue through my face."

I believe some places around where I live, people believe that the moon landing was fake and wrestling is real.

A little (or maybe a lot) of sake with Bob Orton Jr. in Japan

Bob Teaches Me to Swing Like the Babe

Bob Orton Jr. was on his forty-first trip to the Orient on my first trip there. Bob came up to me after my second match and asked me how long I had been wrestling. I told him two weeks. He replied that he didn't mean, how long had I been in Japan, but rather how long had I been wrestling. I told him again, two weeks. In disbelief he asked me in his gravelly voice, "Then what are you doing here?"

At that point I wasn't sure why I was there, either.

Bob helped me greatly on that tour. I still, however, had some of the worst matches in Japanese history. Toward the end of the tour I asked Bob how to use a chair. Every night when I would get tired, one of the Japanese wrestlers would invariably grab a chair and hit me over the head. I was beginning to really hate this.

Bob told me that using a chair was easy—just pick it up and swing it like Babe Ruth. A lot of wrestlers have been upset that I ever got that advice.

There are times when things snowball on you, and you end up over your head. This happened to me in Japan. It also has happened to a lot of day traders and those that felt they knew more they did and foolishly risked their money based on just a little knowledge. However, when it happens to you and your money, then it is a troublesome thing.

Remember, you work too hard for your money not to invest it properly.

The Fair Disclosure Act

The Fair Disclosure Act was meant to ensure that everyone receives information at the same time, from the big investment firms to the average investor. The problem is that the big firms regularly monitor these press releases, while the average investors do not have time to be aware of all the things that are going on in the market because of work obligations. It is not a matter of intelligence, but rather a matter of time and priorities. The average person works and therefore does not have the time to follow the market as closely as someone who follows the market as a profession.

Even though the Fair Disclosure Act was supposed to ensure that every individual would have the same advantage that the professional money managers have, that is still not the case. While the Fair Disclosure Act has helped even the playing field, only so much can be done. A professional money manager who owns a million shares of a company's stock has certain advantages. For instance, she will be able to pick up the phone and call that company direct to talk to someone of importance about the direction of the company. The average investor will not be able to do this. While the professional money manager may not get any more information than you will through various mediums, she will be able to hear tone of voice and have interaction with the company directly. This is still a huge advantage.

Leave trading and speculating to the professionals. I can guarantee you that you will be much happier that way. Investing long-term can be done by anyone, with a little effort. Trading on a regular basis is best left up to the professionals, who have the advantage.

Buy Low, Sell High

The wrong way to invest in the stock market is to see a stock that has had a great run-up and believe that you have to get in on the stock before it goes up any further. When people do this, they are strictly following momentum. This can be effective for a short-term trader, but it can also get a short-term trader burned very badly.

When people follow momentum, they are simply buying a stock because the price is going up. Remember, you are buying a company when you buy stock. The way to get a good deal on a company is not to buy it when prices are inflated.

Simply buy low and sell high.

It sounds like I am being too simple when I state, "Buy low and sell high." However, this is the basis of any type of free market, *if* you want to make money. It can be called being a contrarian, or just being smart.

Buying stock in a company is buying that company. There is no reason not to wait until it goes on sale (the stock price goes down) to buy it.

If you are driving down the road, and you see gasoline for a dollar a gallon and you know that in 100 miles it will be two dollars, it is silly not to buy the gas now. You know you will need the gas sooner or later. Buy it on sale.

It is the same way with the stock market. When you are looking at a company that you want to own, the stock price goes down, and it is not due to fundamental changes in the company, then you are getting the chance to buy that company on sale.

They call this contrarian investing, because you are acting contrary to what the market is doing. I call it buying low and selling high.

With mutual funds and index funds, the decision is much easier. You don't have to worry about individual companies. You are buying into a majority of the market, so why buy when it is high? Buy on sale. Dollar-cost averaging eliminates all of the thinking from the equation, because you have decided to buy the same amount each month.

The market is referred to as the great discounter. By the time you hear news about a stock, it is usually figured into the stock price. If a company comes out with either good or bad news, then that news is immediately figured into the stock price. So by the time you get a hot tip on a stock or see a stock featured in a magazine, so has everyone else. This is why you have to stick to the fundamentals of companies and buy good companies for the long term.

There are many people who see a stock have a good run-up and think they have to get in right away, or else they will be losing money. The problem is, whatever news or momentum is driving the stock up has already been figured into the price. The stock market generally looks ahead about six months—this is why future earnings estimates are so important.

Viagra Versus Compounding Interest

Albert Einstein stated that the greatest invention of modern man is compounding interest. Of course, Viagra was not around then.

Investing long-term allows compounding interest to work. Trading stocks does not.

Not investing long-term means you sell stocks periodically. By selling stocks periodically, you must pay taxes on your profits instead of letting your entire profit work for you in a compounding way.

If you are selling your stocks, you must be selling winners. The problem with selling a winner—and believe me, you never go wrong taking a profit—is that you must have a better place to put your money. If the stock still has legs, then you are losing money by selling the stock. Capital gains, the rate at which you pay taxes on your profit, can be a huge factor. Currently, when you own a stock at least a year, you will only pay 20 percent tax on the profit. On any stock you sell that has been owned less than a year, you will pay your regular tax rate. This should make a difference in how long you hold the stock.

It is important to know that tax reasons are not good reasons to sell or hold on to a stock. Worry about making money. If you are making money in the stock market, you will have money to pay your taxes. Tax breaks should not be your main concern when deciding to sell or buy a stock.

Your main focus is to make money, period.

If you are getting stuck on taxes and have to find a way to sell stock to get a break on them, then the problem is not your taxes. It is your lack of planning toward taxes. Don't lose the effect of compounding interest because your tax planning was poor.

Compounding interest is easy to understand. The Viagra, you will have to figure out on your own. That's a different book, and one that I won't be writing. At least not until I get a little older.

Summary

- Learn English from a handbook.

- Buy-and-hold doesn't mean buy-and-ignore.

- If you have a tree in your yard, do not invite Brad Rheingans over.

- You work too hard for your money not to invest it properly.

CHAPTER | 8

SNAPPLE DOESN'T FOAM, AND YOU DON'T SIP WATER

Don't Follow the Blind

Television days at World Wrestling Entertainment are typically long. We have to arrive early and are often there late. On one of these long days, I noticed that my APA tag team partner and very good friend Ron Simmons was drinking a bottle of Snapple. I had never noticed him drinking Snapple before, so I looked closer.

I noticed the Snapple was foaming.

Now, I *know* Snapple doesn't foam.

We weren't working this day at TV, but as a matter of respect and interest, we were staying to watch the show. Things change so quickly, it is always a good idea to hang around in case you are needed. With a 100 percent injury rate in this business, changes in the roster and the television show may occur by the minute. So while you may not be scheduled to work a certain night, that can always change any second.

After watching Ron for a while, I finally realized that he had found some of Steve Austin's beer and had poured it into a Snapple bottle. He was drinking a beer and watching the show on the monitor in the backstage area, and no one noticed what he was doing. I realized then why he was the brain of our team.

Ever wonder why I respect Ron so much? I used to just try and steal Steve's beer; Ron was drinking it in front of him. Ron's a lot smarter than me.

Picking companies to invest in is much the same as looking at that Snapple bottle. Just because it looks one way on the outside does not mean it's the same on the inside. You have to "look past the door," as my friend Mutt used to say. You might *think* something is Snapple, but you have to look a little deeper.

Companies can have a great public relations campaign and make themselves look very attractive. This is why you have to *Look Past the Door.*

Pleasing shareholders is a big concern to most companies. The management of these companies will have their jobs at stake when things are going wrong. The shareholders are the ones that usually start asking for the actual heads of management first. This is one reason why companies, especially companies that are not in good financial shape, really use their marketing guys to maintain a good image. You have to look past this. This isn't hard to do—you just have to look at their *numbers* and not their *marketing campaign.*

These companies can also use very creative accounting to better their bottom line. While it is certainly not always illegal, creative accounting may be misleading at first glance. It is necessary to always look past the door. I am definitely not saying that a lot of companies are purposely trying to be misleading. These companies must have a marketing campaign to lure consumers. You have to understand the difference—when you are an investor—between the hype and good solid fundamentals.

Jake the Snake and the Pope Mobile

Being in the business that I am in, I sometimes find it easier to spot things that aren't as they seem. Jake "The Snake" Roberts was one of these things. I really believe a four-year-old could have figured him out. However, he did fool a lot of people.

Jake was getting toward the end of his career when he decided to become religious. However, like most of Jake's life, this was a complete scam. Jake would book himself on the religious talk circuit, spout the one speech he had learned, and make a lot of money. However, Jake still enjoyed wild living. He was just more discreet about it.

Jake somehow got stuck with me on a Canadian trip along with Mick Foley and Ron Simmons. As we were coming back from Lethbridge to Calgary, Canada, we stopped to get us some adult beverages for everyone but Mick, who was driving. About fifteen minutes after leaving the store, Jake turned to talk to

Mick. His words were slurring so badly you could barely understand him. Jake hadn't had an adult beverage yet, so the only thing we can figure is that when he went to the bathroom in the store, he somehow found a way to get to a state of nirvana very quickly.

After about an hour, Jake asked Mick to pull over so he could go to the bathroom. Mick asked him if he thought the pope had the pope mobile pull over on the way to Rome so that he could take a leak also. Jake didn't find this very funny; however, he didn't straighten up either. Companies—like people—sometimes are not what they portray themselves to be.

With companies and with people, you have to look beyond the door, because it is easy to be fooled if you don't.

My daddy used to tell me that you don't have to worry about the guy that threatens to beat you up. Worry about the guy that shows up on your doorstep, looking for a fight.

As everywhere, there is always a lot of big talk in the corporate world. It is important to listen with a discerning ear. There are certain ways to know if a company is a good company to invest in. *Remember, if you buy stock in a company, you are buying part of the company.* So buy stock in companies you want to own. If you enjoy shopping at Wal-Mart and everyone you know enjoys shopping there also, this could be a good stock to own. If you see a company growing by leaps and bounds, this could be a good stock to own. As Peter Lynch, one of the greatest investors of our time, is famous for saying, "Know what you own."

Just as bigotry among the educated is very rare, so is paranoia about buying stocks among those who understand the market. Ever since the crash of 1929, and the bubble burst of the last few years, a stigma has been associated with the stock market among some. Once you begin to know what you own, these fears are shown to be baseless.

I believe the same as Peter Lynch—that you can spot trends and hot items by simply observing what is happening around you. When you walk into a mall, notice what people are buying and what stores are always full. Notice what people are driving. Whenever you spot a trend or hot item, then you can do the fundamental research to see what to invest in to best benefit from this trend.

Warren Buffett, who is arguably the greatest investor of all time, never invested in technology because he didn't feel like he knew enough about it to invest in it. It is wise not to invest in a company that you do not fully understand. Stay with what you know.

Dutch Mantel and me. I don't know if Dutch drove as badly as Tom, since he never drove.

Don't Fight Sober

I learned a lesson one night in Philadelphia from a very good left hook. That left hook taught me to stay with my strengths.

One summer WWE decided to have a tough-man contest among its wrestlers, a legit athletic contest where nothing would be scripted. The contest would be a tournament format, with fights consisting of three rounds. The fighters would wear boxing gloves, and wrestling takedowns were legal.

A lot of our guys are very tough individuals, but had little formal training in an organized combat sport like boxing. This actually makes the fights more entertaining. The best fights are the ones that involve two tough people who want to fight but aren't really good at it. I fit into this category. In fact, just like several of the guys in the tournament, I had never put on a pair of boxing gloves before. I did pretty well in the tournament and made it to the finals. It was a very strange thing, though. Most fights involve a quick punch and rolling around a parking lot, trying to get a finger in someone's eye and hoping that one of his friends doesn't put his cowboy boot in your ear. Now here I was fighting some of my best friends, and both of us were sober. It was definitely a unique experience.

There were some tough guys in this tournament: Charles Wright (the Godfather), Steve "Dr. Death" Williams, Don Harris, Darren Drozdov, Henry Godwinn, Too Cold Scorpio, Bob "Hardcore" Holly, and several others. However, the two best fighters were Bart Gunn and Steve Blackman. Blackman was in my bracket, but he blew out his knee training for the second fight. In his first fight he showed what happens when a good wrestler meets a good boxer. He absolutely humiliated former Golden Gloves champion Marc Mero. With Steve out, though, I was confident I could make it to the finals.

I fought Darren Drozdov in the semifinals in an extremely close fight. Darren hit very hard. We were both tired from having to fight the night before, and neither one of us put on our best performance.

Later in the season, Darren was dropped onto his head during a wrestling maneuver in Nassau Coliseum, paralyzing him from the neck down. Darren and I have hunted together in Alabama. He loves to hunt. I look forward to the day that Darren will get up out of his wheelchair and walk. I know he will. I fought him. I know how tough he is. I just hope he doesn't want a rematch— he hits too hard. We'll just go hunting together instead.

I really thought I would be fighting my good friend Charles Wright in the final, but I don't think anyone had any idea how hard Bart Gunn could hit. Bart and Charles had a great fight, but Charles made the same mistake I would make the following week. It wasn't forgetting to duck Bart's left hook—it was fighting sober. I don't believe either one of us ever had done that.

I should have stayed with what I knew, and what I knew certainly wasn't boxing. I was used to fighting with country music playing in the background, sawdust on the floor, and a mechanical bull in the back.

Country-and-western bars put sawdust on the floors so that the folks who like to boot scoot (dance) can dance easier. It is a hard thing to fight on a sawdust floor; I have seen many a cowboy fall trying to throw a punch. I had become quite the expert on sawdust-floor fighting. While it's not necessarily a great thing to be good at, it does help you to survive the onslaught of a drunken redneck.

Now I don't want to take anything from Bart winning, nor make excuses. Bart was better than me that night. I just think my chances would have been better on my home turf instead of Bart's. It certainly would have been more fun.

The lesson I learned was simple: stay with your strengths. Or, more simply put—don't fight sober.

A little knowledge can be a harmful thing. There is nothing worse than a first-year psychology student. They think they know it all. Give them a few years. Usually, the more knowledge you have, the more you realize you don't have a handle on everything. That's a much healthier outlook.

With Ken Shamrock, the greatest UFC fighter of all time, and Sean Waltman.

I had trained for a couple of weeks for my last fight with Guy Mezger, a four-time world kick-boxing champion and a very good trainer out of Dallas, Texas. Guy actually commented to me one day that I was getting a lot better. I asked how he could possibly know, since I hadn't hit him in two weeks. He said I was getting closer.

The problem I had was that, like most first-year psychology students, I now thought I knew something about boxing. This would prove to be very wrong.

I make light about the fact that I lost that fight. Don't get me wrong, though. Losing that fight was the worst night of my life. I would rather have died in that ring than to have lost. Bart is a good fighter and a good guy, but I never dreamed I would lose. It has haunted me ever since, almost daily at times. Ken Shamrock, the best no-holds-barred fighter in the world, told me that the only person who has not lost a fight is one who has not fought long enough. I understand that, but I still don't like it.

That is what happens when something means a lot to you and you fail. You can either quit—which is not an option, in my opinion—or you can get up and keep going. Of course, I still don't plan on fighting sober, though. Stay with your strengths.

A little knowledge about the stock market has lost a lot of money for a lot of people. People find out a few things about companies or get hot tips off TV, don't research these things, and make unwise decisions.

Potential Don't Pay the Rent

My high school football coach, W. T. (any coach that goes by his initials has to be tough—and he was) Stapler, used to tell me that I had potential. Then he would explain to me that "potential" meant that so far I hadn't done anything.

Seeing a company you like means that the stock has potential, but you must do a little research to see if that company has done anything worth investing in. And if a good-looking (it's my book, I can write that if I want to) professional wrestler can figure out how to invest in the stock market, I promise that with just a little effort you can, too. The key is to invest in what you know.

It is extremely important not to invest in anything you don't understand. You wouldn't do this in any other area of your life. Why do it with your retirement?

If you can't describe what exactly the company that you want to invest in does, you shouldn't invest in it.

Look Past the Share Price

The first thing to realize when looking at stocks is that *share price in and of itself is not indicative of how much a company is worth.* Every company issues a certain number of shares. The share price depends greatly on how many shares are outstanding, or how many shares are in the market for purchase.

For example, if for simple math reasons company A has 10 shares outstanding and company B has 100 shares outstanding, then these two companies are valued completely differently if the stock price of both is $10.

Company A would have a market capitalization of $100 ($10 share price × 10 outstanding shares). Company B would have a market capitalization of $1,000 ($10 share price × 100 outstanding shares). You can see that just because the share price of a company seems very high, this doesn't mean that the stock is either expensive or cheap based solely on the price.

It would be the same thing as four people buying into a local company and paying $100 apiece. These four people have each purchased a share in this company. Now if the same company was offered to eight people paying $100 a piece, then these eight are paying twice what the four paid for the exact same company. Even though the first group and the second group paid the same amount per share, the second group was paying twice what they should because of the difference in the number of shares.

Leaders and Laggards

Two words used to describe companies are *leader* and *laggard.*

Always stick with leaders. There are 10,000 stocks available;

don't waste your money on bad ones. Why invest in less than the best when you have a choice? There are good reasons that these companies are leaders; they generally make a lot of money. You want to invest in companies that make a lot of money.

Laggards can have a cheaper stock price, but there is a reason they are cheap. You have a choice of 10,000 companies. Don't buy a bad company. This is your money.

You should definitely buy a company that is a good company when its stock price is down. This is a smart thing to do. This is buying a good company at a discount.

Always buy leaders.

PE Ratio

One of the things that is discussed so much among stock pickers is price-to-earnings ratio. Price-to-earnings ratio is not the only way to evaluate the value of a company, but it is a good start. It is one of many factors to be considered.

Price-to-earnings ratio, or PE, is easily calculated: divide the price of the stock by the earnings per share (EPS).

Now stay with me. This is when a lot of people quit reading and turn to the end of financial books. But this isn't like most books; I will explain to you what all of these phrases mean. So please stick with me here. This is actually very simple.

If company A has 100 shares of stock, and it makes $100 profit for the year, then the earnings per share (EPS) would be $1. That is, the earnings divided by the total EPS would be $1. ($100 profit ÷ 100 shares = $1 per share.) If this same company had a share price of $30, then the PE (price-to-earnings ratio) would be 30. That is the share price divided by the EPS (earnings per share).

If company B also had 100 shares, but it earned $200, then the EPS would be $2—the total earnings ($200) divided by the total number of shares (100). If the share price on this company were also $30, then the PE would be 15, because the share price of 30 is now divided by the EPS, which is $2.

Here are two companies with the same share price, yet valued completely differently by the market. Company B you can acquire (based exclusively on the PE) at half price compared to company A. This is certainly not the only way to evaluate a company, but it can be one way to get a snapshot of how the company is evaluated right now by the market.

Remember that we are looking solely at how the company is evaluated right now. While you can determine a lot about a company by looking at its past and present, one of the most important factors when investing in a company is determining where the company is headed. But beware. Even with all of the great analysts out there giving forward-looking estimates, they are still giving estimates.

However, you can look at a company and see part of the horizon. If company B, which is valued at a significant discount to company A, is making eight-track tapes right when the cassette is coming out, you might see storm clouds on the horizon. Company B might have been a great earner making eight-track tapes, but it may not have prepared for the future boom of the cassette. In this case the future of company B might be bleak compared to company A, even though currently it trades at a huge discount. Remember, forward-looking estimates are still speculation, although very educated speculation.

Fat Potential and Future Growth in Stocks

You can see how a company has grown historically, and very accurately, by looking at its PE and EPS growth for the last five years. History has a way of repeating itself. When you first meet your sweetheart and go home to meet her parents, if you realize that everyone related to her is well over 300 pounds, I would be wary. There is a chance your sweetheart will sprout as well. College kids call this "FP," short for fat potential.

Looking at history can be very useful. Companies that have shown good, consistent growth will (unless something has changed) generally continue to show good, consistent growth.

A PE ratio is also good to determine if a stock is overpriced relative to what it has done historically. You can look up a stock's historic range with its PE ratio. When the stock moves out of this range, the move should send up a red flag to you as a possible sell signal.

My Three-Dollar Night

It is very important to see sequential growth in EPS. I remember when I first started wrestling in Dallas, Texas. My first match was at the Villa Inn in Garland, Texas, part of the Dallas/Fort Worth area. I was so excited to start wrestling, even though it was in a shabby, run-down bar. I was proud . . . until I got paid. It was all of $10. I had driven an hour and a half each way, gotten beaten up and bruised, all for $10.

The next match I had was the main event match at the Sportatorium in Dallas, where I wrestled Rod Price for the heavyweight championship. I got $25 for that night. Of course, there were only approximately 2,000 people there. My earnings were growing sequentially. However, so was how I was getting screwed.

The good news is, sequential growth in companies is a good way to recognize consistent growth; the only thing I was recognizing in wrestling was that promoters can be crooks. I would love to mention names of some of the worst crooks, like Iceman King Parsons, who paid me THREE dollars one night, but I won't.

Historic PE Ranges

A company generally stays within its historic PE range. During the bull run of the late 1990s when everything was becoming overvalued, historic PE range would have been a great indicator that stocks were out of their normal range. Once these stocks start getting out of their normal range, it is worth taking a second look at them. If a stock has traditionally had a PE of 15–20 and a recent run-up has caused it to jump to a PE of 25–30, then it is worth taking a second look to examine the reason for the run-up. If there is not a logical reason except that momentum has taken it out of its historical range, then you should be wary.

Remember that just because a stock is going up, that does not mean that it will continue to go up. It is better to buy near the bottom than the top. That sounds simple and basic—and it is—but a lot of people end up chasing a stock. Chasing a stock is something that happens when emotions get involved in stock picking.

The year I coached at Trinity Valley Community College we were 2 and 8. That's why I no longer coach.

Cutting Players and Picking Stocks

I coached one year at Trinity Valley Community College in Athens, Texas, for a great man and coach, Carl Andress. Being a small junior college, we had just a certain number of roster spots open, and we had to cut several players. We were so small that we had to give our only helmet to the guy who was carrying the ball. This usually gave away our game plan. (Okay, we weren't that poor.)

It was a hard thing to do to a young man just out of high school. This was the only part I hated about coaching. It was an extremely hard thing to tell a young man who has most likely never failed at anything that he is not good enough to make the team. Unfortunately, this is life. But I still agonized over the decisions.

Coach Andress used to tell me all the time to distance myself from the players because I had to make decisions that were best for the team and that were fair. If I became too close to the players before the cut date, I might make a decision based on emotion, not good judgment.

Picking and deciding whether to hold on to stocks is exactly the same. People become emotionally attached to these stocks and are tempted to make unsound decisions. People that have held a stock for a long time hate to get rid of that stock even if the fundamentals change. *You have to keep emotion out of stock picking.* This will also help eliminate the urge to chase a stock.

PEG—PE-to-Growth Ratio

A PE-to-growth ratio of 1 is a very good ratio. For example, if the PE is 15 and the estimated growth rate is 15 percent, divide the PE into the estimated growth ratio. This gives you a quotient of 1—a very good number. Anything under 1 is considered very good. The higher you get over 1, the more volatile the stock will be (and the better chance the stock is overvalued). This quotient of 1 is what many mutual fund managers like to have when investing in a company.

A company that has a PE of 20 and has projected earnings of more than 20 percent has a PEG (price-to-earnings-to-growth ratio) of less than 1 (PE ÷ projected earnings = PEG). Remember, although this is a very educated estimate, these projected future numbers are estimates that can change.

When a company has a PE of 30 and a growth ratio of 60 percent (which would give you a PEG of 2), this is where speculation almost begins. The reason is that the estimates are high, which is the cause of the rich PE, but you are pricing perfection into the companies' price. Any little falter below these high estimates, and the stock could experience a big downward move. This is why you have to realize that while these estimates are usually fairly accurate, they can still be wrong.

The stocks of companies with high projected growth rates are the stocks that are traditionally highly volatile.

ROE—Return on Equity

ROE (return on equity) is something everyone looks at when valuing an investment, though they may not call it that. ROE is simply how much you are making on the money or assets you have in a venture.

There wasn't a lot to do while growing up in Sweetwater, Texas, except play football and hunt rattlesnakes. Sweetwater is the home of the world's largest rattlesnake roundup, and catching snakes and selling them to the local Jaycees for their roundup is a good way for kids to make money.

If you invest $50 in snake tongs to grab the snakes and bags in which to put the snakes, *then that $50 is your equity stake.* Say you catch 10 snakes for a total of 30 pounds, and that brings you $300, given that the snakes are worth $10 a pound. *The $300 would be your return on equity,* a 500 percent return.

Most stocks return an average around 12 percent, but with stocks you don't have the chance of getting bitten by a poisonous viper.

If a snake hunter in West Texas understands return on equity, I promise you can, too. ROE can be an important measure of how a company uses its resources. ROE is basically how a company is making good use of its assets.

You simply look at how much the company has in equity and divide it by its earnings. A return of around 15 percent is a good return, but remember, compare apples to apples. Compare stocks of the same sector against each other.

There are many things to look at when buying a stock. One of the main things to bear in mind is that you don't have to memorize a bunch of benchmarks and standards when looking at stocks. What I mean by this is that you don't have to remember that 15 is a good PE for a retail stock or that 16–17 is a good return on equity (ROE) for a growth stock. You can compare companies' numbers to those of other companies and even to certain indices relative to these stocks. You can do this very easily on many Internet sites, which will give you a good indication of how these stocks are priced compared to other companies in the same sector.

Price to Sales and Price to Cash Flow

Price to sales and price to cash flow are also very important indicators of a company's performance capabilities. Compare the companies with each other to see how they stack up.

The Internet has several sites where you can put in a company's symbol and compare it within the sector it is in, within the broader market, or just to another company.

Company Debt

One thing that is sometimes overlooked by the average investor is how much debt a company has on its books. People get so accustomed to looking at forward earnings that many times "cash on hand" and debt are ignored. This is one of the main things to show how solvent a company is in any economic climate. In a terrific bull market, every company can look good. It is when the bull has been gored and times are tough that a company's true mettle shows.

How much cash a company has can be very important in an unstable-interest-rate environment. With interest rates rising and falling, a company like Microsoft that has more than $50 billion in cash and investments at its disposal has very little to worry about. The companies that don't have cash on hand are the ones that can be in trouble. Looking at a company's debt load is very important.

To make debt more easily understood, look at a few personal examples.

For example, say you are earning $100,000 a year, and you have credit card and other debt of $250,000. Now say your neighbor earns just $75,000 a year but has no debt. Who is better positioned for the future? You make a third more than your neighbor, yet you are saddled with debt. If you had a choice, who would you invest in, you or your neighbor? It is the same with companies.

Jeff Bezos, the leader of Amazon.com, is apparently a great CEO. However, even when the company starts consistently making a profit, Amazon and Bezos will still have the problem of the mountains of debt because he borrowed to build his company. I love shopping on Amazon. It is one of the best shopping web sites I have found, and is extremely easy to navigate. Mr. Bezos has built a great company that is fun to do business with. However, I would not recommend investing in a company that has that much debt—at least, not yet.

I always thought that companies like Amazon did things backward. They built the brand name first. They then realized they did not have a nationwide distribution channel, so they had to build this channel. This meant building distribution centers all over the United States. This drove these companies to debt problems and a bunch of buildings, which the Internet was supposed to eliminate.

I believe that the best way to utilize the Internet was and is to take a company like Wal-Mart or Barnes & Noble (both of which so far have not been very successful with their Internet presence) that already has a distribution channel nationwide and then build a Web presence. If a company like these two had hired a smart guy like Mr. Bezos to build its web presence, then it would have been extremely successful.

I think you will see this happen in the near future. I believe that it will be possible to order something on-line from one of these nationwide chains in the morning and have it delivered to you in the afternoon. This is what will happen when these nationwide chains figure out what Mr. Bezos already has. At the time you order something, the local Wal-Mart will deliver it to you that day. Sound far-fetched? Look at what has happened over the past ten years, and you will believe not only that it is possible but that it will happen.

The reason I bring this up is because I want you, when you look at companies to invest in, to look at the whole picture. *Look past the door.* Very few people would have missed the fact that these Internet companies lacked the infrastructure to be successful if they had just taken a step back and looked at these companies logically. However, thousands of people were fooled and lost a ton of money because of their lack of foresight.

PEs, PEGs, and debt are certainly important things to explore. And if you had looked closely at these things you would not have been burned by the dot-com mania. These companies didn't even have a PE ratio because they never had an E (earnings) to go with the P (price). They only had the P.

There is no such thing as a price ratio for a very good reason. Sometimes you can be so close that you will miss the forest for the trees. This happens when you start number-crunching too much. Number-crunching never hurts. It is a very good thing in which to excel. However, don't get so caught up in numbers you miss the trends of our society.

Fuzzy Math

The saying, "Figures never lie, but figures do," is very accurate. I am certainly not calling anyone a liar (with the exception of a few people at Enron and Worldcom) about accounting practices, but there are several legal "creative" ways to manufacture numbers. This is why it is very important to look past the door.

For instance, they say that 50 percent of marriages end in divorce. One of the ways they get this number is by taking all of the new marriage certificates this year and dividing them by all of the divorce decrees this year. Sounds reasonable, but look past the door.

Say 100 couples get married each year. Now, if 50 couples get divorced this year, is that half of the couples that got married this year? No. Most couples take longer than a year to realize that they hate each other. If 100 couples have gotten married every year for the past 10 years, then you have 1,000 married couples (100 per year × 10 years). The divorces are of 50 of the couples that have been married over the past 10 years or however long—at least 1,000 couples. Now the number has dropped dramatically. So, the statistics now could read that only 50 out of 1,000 couples get divorced, which is only 5 percent. I don't believe this number is accurate either, I believe it is somewhere in between. But this is how numbers can be manipulated.

Be careful to look at the bottom line in companies and make comparisons to companies also in their sector. Numbers like cash on hand and outstanding debt are hard (but not impossible, as we have found out) to lie about.

The Mysterious "Goodwill"

One of the ways that companies manipulate their numbers is through what is called goodwill. Goodwill is the difference between book value and the amount a company paid to acquire another company. When a company buys another company, the companies agree on a price for the sale. Now the company that is being acquired has to be valued at a certain figure. One of the ways to value a company is called book value. *Book value is the combined assets of the company minus its debt.* Book value is basically the bottom line that you found out about yourself in chapter 1 by filling out the worksheet. It works the same for companies. Once you understand a little simple accounting, then you understand that it is universal. The same accounting that works for small accounts works for large companies, only in bigger numbers.

Goodwill is the difference between book value (a company's bottom line worth) of the company being acquired and what the acquiring company paid for the company. If company A is worth $9 million in book value and company B pays $10 million, then the goodwill would be the difference, which is $1 million.

What these companies do with this goodwill charge is where the shady accounting can come into play. First, you might ask why a company would pay more than book value for a company. It is because you have no way of valuating potential. Company B would be paying what it believes is fair market value based on what the company could be worth, which would be above book value.

The acquiring companies can amortize this goodwill for as much as forty years, which means that the $1 million difference would cost the company's bottom line just $25,000 a year for forty years. This can be very misleading.

This is why you should look at as many factors as you can before buying stock in a company. Things aren't always as they seem.

Keep It Simple

Remember, Snapple doesn't foam. Look beyond the door.

Also look to the future; it doesn't take a person with a Ph.D. to spot trends. The emergence of DVDs pretty much means the demise of the videocassette. It would not be wise to invest in a pure videotape manufacturing company. This is a trend that anyone can spot if they just use a little common sense.

Think about the Internet boom and subsequent bust. A little foresight would have helped a lot of people keep their money. When you have something new emerge, like the Internet, you need to find a safe way to invest in the boom that will follow.

It was very obvious that few of the companies that started up would succeed; a lot of people were betting hard-earned money that they would be right. It is smarter to buy into companies you know will be around.

No matter who survives and who doesn't, there are several companies that will benefit because of the emergence of the Internet. These are the companies on which the Internet itself is dependent. These companies are the ones that must build and furnish the Internet.

Companies that supply technology and software for web pages will be around. Companies that supply all of the necessary equipment and technologies for the Internet will last and make money no matter which dot-coms make it and which don't.

It is the same with any new technological emergence that creates a whole new business. At the start of the century there were many car manufacturers; few survived. However, if you had invested in supplies needed to build these cars (such as steel), you would have been making a safe bet. No matter who made the car, steel was necessary. Be smart with your money. When in doubt with an emerging technology, invest in the infrastructure that is necessary for that technology to exist.

Common sense and a little work are all that is needed to invest long-term in the equity markets. Know what you own. Your money is too hard to come by to waste it on something about which you are not certain.

One of the best ways to invest in companies is to first list twenty companies or so in which you want to invest, or that you would be interested in investing in if the price were right. Then do a little research on these companies and narrow your field even more. When you have decided on the companies, decide a price at which you would be happy to buy the company. Now wait, watch the market, and when these companies hit these price targets, then you will feel comfortable buying their stock.

Constantly keep your list updated and your buy points (the price you'd pay) updated. This will help ensure that you are buying these companies at a reasonable price.

After your first investment in the equity markets, the learning curve will sharpen dramatically because you now have an interest in the market. So get started.

Day Trading, Futures, Options, and Blackjack

I have purposely left out advice on futures, options, and day trading. I understand that some professionals can make a lot of money trading futures and options. They would probably be very upset at me for including day trading alongside their profession. I apologize to the professionals that feel that way, but I feel that the average investor needs to stay completely away from these three speculative investments.

Futures and options involve speculating on the future. Nostradamus couldn't do this accurately; it is foolish to think that the average person could. I personally wouldn't give my hard-earned money to a professional to invest in these things either. I simply don't believe in the consistent merits of investing in either one. There are way too many companies to invest in where you can be reasonably assured of making money for you to speculate when you don't have to.

As far as day trading goes, don't do it. This is the same thing as going to Las Vegas—a terrific city—and playing blackjack or craps with your money. Now don't get me wrong, I enjoy playing blackjack in Vegas; I just don't do it with money I need for retirement.

Day trading is not based on anything scientific—despite what proponents of it might say. A lot of brokerages make money from day traders because they get a commission on every buy and sell order that comes through. These are the only people making money off day trading.

If you love gambling and must day-trade, I understand that this is America and you have that right. I would just ask you to be sensible about it. Now, that is an oxymoron—a sensible day trader. Only use money you can lose, because you will lose it. But have fun. It usually is fun blowing money until the realization sets in of how foolish you were.

The equity markets are a safe place to put your money. With any investment, a little research needs to be done. This is your money; don't work hard to earn it and then lose it because you don't research where to invest it. This is your future that you are planning, and with a little effort it can be an extremely bright future.

Compare Apples to Apples

What is important now is to put all of this information together to buy a stock. Like I have said, Finance.Yahoo.com is one web site that allows you to compare a stock to the sector it is in, as well as the S&P index, the Dow, other stocks, and a host of other comparisons. When you are trying to determine the value of a stock, comparison shopping can be useful.

Compare how the PE ratio of the stock you want to buy compares to its sector. Compare debt ratios and return on equity to other stocks in its sector. Compare the stock to an index like the S&P 500.

Just remember to compare apples to apples. When you compare stocks from different sectors, you may not get a true picture.

Always remember that it is hard to go wrong with a company that has little debt and good cash flow. After all, that is the kind of business you would want to own. Owning stocks is owning part of a business.

Summary

- Gamble in Vegas; the cocktail waitresses are prettier. Don't gamble in the stock market.

- Don't fight sober.

- Look past the door.

- Potential don't do jack.

- Stock price—in and of itself—does not tell you if the stock is cheap or expensive.

- Little debt + good cash flow = good business.

CHAPTER | 9

PUTTING IT ALL TOGETHER

Making country-western singer Darryl Worley dance on a bunker at Kandahar Airport in Afghanistan while waiting for a flight to Kabul. (Darryl's ground-hog danced also.)

You Plugged Your Leak, Now Chart Your Course

Now comes the fun part: putting it all together.

You have learned in chapters 2 to 4 that the only way to have money is to save money, and the only way to save money is to have money to save. Sound simple? It is.

If you don't have any extra money, there must be a reason. You have a hole in your financial boat. You first have to fix the hole and then worry about the water (your debt). You will never be able to get rid of your debt (water) until you stop the incurrence of debt (the hole in the boat).

You must deal with the problem—not the symptom. Find the problem and eliminate it. Attack it. You must change your lifestyle, not temporarily alter your behavior. Find what is causing your debt and eliminate it. The symptom is the debt; the problem is the incurrence of debt. Remember, attacking the symptom first is akin to giving a person with a brain tumor an aspirin because she has a headache. You must attack the problem for long-term health, which is the tumor.

You must attack the problem of the incurrence of debt to have long-term relief.

Believe me, making more money will not solve your problem. Bad habits have gotten you into this mess. If you make more money and don't alter your habits, you will still spend more than you should. Change your habits.

After you have eliminated what is causing your debt, then, and only then, can you start eliminating the debt that the problem has caused you to accumulate.

You have to have a plan. You must set your goal for being debt-free and work backward from the goal. You cannot just decide one day to get out of debt and never develop a plan. Set a time frame and then figure out how you are going to systematically reduce your debt until it is zero.

Start with your worst debt first. Use the amortization chart in chapter 3, and after setting your time frame, determine how much you have to put toward your debt to eliminate it in a timely fashion. After you have eliminated your worst debt (probably your credit card debt), then go on to your next highest, and so on.

After you have set a plan to get rid of the incurrence of debt and then the debt itself, you must set a systematic and consistent savings plan so you don't have to work your entire life. You may want to work, but it should be your option.

Give yourself a pay cut. Cut your own pay 5 to 10 percent, or whatever you can stand. This is the money you will use to pay off your debt and start saving toward your future—a future that is looking brighter by the day. I promise you won't miss the money. If your boss came in and told you that he was cutting your pay, you would adjust. You would have to. Cut it yourself for the sake of your future. You will adjust, and your life will be better.

Swimming with great white sharks off the coast of South Africa, near Hermanus.

Once you have paid off your debt, then use the money you were paying off your debt with to put in your retirement account. Drive your car ten years, the last five with no payment. Use this payment toward your savings. You are no longer using it toward your car. You are used to not having this money. Don't wait for some pie-in-the-sky dream. Create your own.

Once you have started putting aside money, put it aside wisely. Start with your company retirement plan, if you have one. If you don't, use the SEP (self-employed pension), or one of the IRA plans described in chapter 5. You get tax deductions for this money. It is like getting free money.

If your company has a retirement plan and matches your donation, this is free money also. If you don't take advantage of this, you are being rather dumb. Okay, you are a moron.

Fill up your tax-advantageous accounts first. These accounts are discussed in chapter 5. Then put any extra into a separate retirement account. Remember; always put this money into an account where you can't get it out easily. This way you are not tempted to make an impulse purchase, and therefore deplete your retirement.

Historically, stocks return double what bonds have. Therefore, depending upon your time to retirement (portfolio diversification as it relates to retirement is discussed in chapter 6), you should have most of your money in stocks. There are a variety of ways to invest in stocks, mutual funds, index funds, and individual stocks.

Me with my dear friend Bobby Duncum Jr. at the Sportatorium in Dallas, Texas.

Mutual funds are what most company-based retirement plans are based on, along with index funds. These are two great ways to become very wealthy without a whole lot of work, just a little watchfulness. The S&P 500 index, which is available in most company retirement plans, is a fabulous index to be invested in. Most mutual funds compare their returns to the S&P because it is the benchmark. Sometimes it is simply better to buy the thing everyone is comparing themselves to.

Individual stocks are a great thing to invest in, and I believe if you are investing long-term, anyone can invest in them—as long as you do a little work. Remember, buy and hold, don't buy and ignore. I don't believe in day trading, or speculating. Please leave this to guys who make a living at it. This is a great way to lose a lot of money.

Buy stocks in companies that you want to own, because you

are buying part ownership in these companies. Chapter 8 deals with financial matters to consider. Don't buy on potential. Potential means you ain't done nothing yet. Buy companies that make money, preferably a lot of money. Buy companies that have little debt. Compare the company you are considering purchasing to companies in the same sector. Compare apples to apples.

Inside Buckingham Palace, serving drinks in Queen Elizabeth's bar. The trip was set up by William Regal.

Whether in funds or individual stocks, buy leaders, not laggards. Keep your portfolio in proportion; don't be overweight in any one sector. Re-allocate your assets annually. Chapter 6 deals with these matters.

You work hard for your money; be smart with it. Work a little to know that the money you have worked so hard for is invested like you want it to be. Use an accredited financial adviser if you want, but remember, this is your money, and he works for you. Know what your money is doing.

Social Security may not be around when you retire, and if it is, you may not get all the benefits you think you will. Prepare for your future. Plan on where you will be five, ten, or twenty years from now and start charting your course. Only you will be to blame if you don't make it.

CHAPTER | 10

DRIVE IT LIKE YOU STOLE IT

Standing on the world-famous Swilcan Bridge at St. Andrew's Golf Course, Scotland, the home of golf.

Go forward twenty or thirty years. Where do you want to be and what do you want to be doing?

Now look back at the twenty or thirty years that you just passed over in your Stephen Hawking time machine. How do you want to be remembered?

One of my goals is that thirty years from now there will be a rowdy card game with all my buddies, and they will be griping about the fact that they can't explain why I have so much money. I hope they are *really* mad, especially since they didn't invite me.

Odds are, you won't make as much money as Bill Gates. So all you have are your memories, your impressions on others, and your happiness. Unfortunately, I have had many good friends die young. I don't like this because I miss them all very much, especially my good friend Bobby Duncum Jr. These deaths have taught me that when you are gone, you are gone. All that is left is how you have influenced people. When you die, you leave it all, whether a little or a lot. All that really matters is what you have done. Please be someone who has done something in life.

In the great movie *Gladiator,* the lead character says that what we do now echoes for eternity. I believe that. You should be someone worthwhile and do something worthwhile.

My Old Truck

My APA tag team partner and best friend, Ron Simmons, has stated that no matter *when* we go, people will have to say that we have spun our tires. We both have driven our trucks like we stole them. I have remodeled an old truck for which my good friend and NASCAR driver Hermie Sadler built a motor. Now, believe me, I have tested that motor. You can ask my neighbors. Ron also has several old cars and trucks. In fact, I think he has as many vehicles as I have boots—and I have a lot of boots. You can ask Atlanta if Ron hasn't enjoyed his vehicles. Remember, life is about living.

At the Great Wall of China with Cindy.

List Your Goals

Make a list of your goals. Write down all of the things you want to accomplish or acquire. Believe me, if you don't know what you want, you won't get it. Once you have made the list, then start determining how to accomplish those things. From small things to big things—write them all down. Some may seem impossible, but you never know until you try. If you don't have any goals, you won't reach them.

Think of your own eulogy. What do you want said about you? Will you have lived your whole life without accomplishing anything? Or will you have died doing exactly what you wanted to do in life? Life is about living, not just existing.

There are many people out there who are so scared of failing that they will never try anything hard or new. These people basically just exist in life. Odds are, you won't notice these people because they never *do* anything. The problem with trying something or caring about something is you could fail at it. If you really care, and fail, then it will hurt.

Don't Be Scared

There is one sure way to not fail and not get hurt. That is to never try. Your eulogy will be really short also, because you will not have done anything in your life. What if Michael Jordan had missed that last second shot against Utah in his final NBA game (that is, before he unretired in 2001)? Would it have hurt him? Of course. But, he didn't miss. That is the other option. You can succeed. When you care about something so much that it is worth risking failure, success is that much sweeter. If there is no risk in something, there is not much reward. Plan on being a success in life. Plan on being willing to put everything on the line. It is a good feeling to care enough to risk failure.

My senior year in college we had the opportunity to play for the Lone Star Conference championship against Texas A&I— now renamed Texas A&M Kingsville. Abilene Christian had suffered through a couple of lean years footballwise, and I knew that this would be the last chance in a long time for a conference championship. I certainly knew that this would be *my* last chance, because this was my senior year. The group that I came in with as a freshman had worked four years to get to this point. A championship was within our grasp.

This game was to be something special for me personally as well. John Randle was Texas A&I's best lineman. In fact, he was the best Division II lineman that year, and the year before as well. John was one of those once-in-a-decade linemen that colleges live to recruit. He had done some phenomenal things on the football field and had received many well-deserved honors. John would later become a great all-pro for the Minnesota Vikings.

The year before, we had played Texas A&I in their home of Kingsville, Texas. They had thoroughly embarrassed us. John Randle was a huge part of that. I believe he had three quarter-back sacks that game. We not only lost the game, we had a bench-clearing brawl at the end of the game that we lost also. I was beginning to wonder if A&I was just going to shoot us. They had done everything else to us.

I did not get to play against John that year because I played right offensive tackle, and he was left defensive end. Randle won conference honors that year of Lineman of the Year, along with consensus All-American honors. I had won all-conference honors and was named to the second team All-American team. Randle was named first team.

I did not feel there was much challenge left for me in the conference except John Randle. To play against him the next year, I would have to switch to left tackle. So I switched to left tackle for the sole purpose of getting to play against such a great player. I wanted to win Lineman of the Year honors. I knew that the only way to do that was to play and do well against the best lineman in the nation. I looked forward to the challenge.

My senior year started badly, with another knee surgery during two-a-days. It looked like I was going to miss the whole season, but then my knee started to come around. Sixteen days after the knee surgery that I thought would sideline me for the season, I was back on the football field. I had already missed two games and didn't play very well in the third one. But then my knee felt better, and I was feeling very good about the way I was playing.

We had had a surprisingly good year. By the time we were to play Texas A&I, we had a chance for the conference championship. I was finally getting to do what I had waited a year to do—play against Randle. I was also surprised that we were in a position to be playing for a championship because Texas A&I had a superior team. This would work to our advantage; A&I almost overlooked us, because they were headed to the play-offs.

I began the game very well. Randle's famous for getting to the quarterback, and so far I had stopped him. He was living up to his reputation of being a great player. You can just feel the difference when you are out there against someone who can play the game well.

In the second quarter, we had a chance to go ahead with our first lead of the game. We were close to the goal, and as usual, Coach Payne decided to run the play behind me to try to score. I went head up with Randle and thought we had a chance to score when I felt something crash into my leg. My leg snapped. The running back had been tripped up in the backfield. His helmet hit my knee brace, and the impact broke my fibula, the small bone of the leg. I found out later that my knee brace had been improperly fitted. For the first time after a knee surgery, my orthopedic surgeon, Dr. Holloway, had not been the one to fit me for my brace. It had been a local physical therapist who thought he knew what he was doing. The impact and the misfit brace caused my leg to break.

To say I was at a crossroads was an understatement. Here was my last chance for a championship and my only chance against Randle—a chance for which I had waited a year.

While I was on the sidelines, my dad came out of the stands for the first time in my career to check on me. My dad, I could take. Now if my mom had come, that might have been too much. Dad asked me what I was going to do. I told him that I planned on finding out how tough I was. Dr. Holloway put a brace on my ankle that prevented the foot from moving, and I went back in the game to finish. I really didn't see any other option. To this day I don't see any other option.

I had lost all mobility in my left leg. After halftime, the swelling had increased, and it was painful to plant that foot. I gave up a

The day I played on a broken leg, my senior year at ACU. I played the next week as well.

quarterback sack to Randle in the third quarter, which was really very upsetting. It was even more upsetting that we lost the last chance I had for a championship in college. Now please don't think that the only reason I gave up a sack to John was because of the broken leg. It could have happened anyway. He was a great player. I just wished I could have finished the game healthy, because it meant so much to me.

Randle made Lineman of the Year again, and we were both consensus All-Americans. John has had a great career with the Minnesota Vikings, and the Seattle Seahawks and I couldn't be happier for him. He came to a couple of our WWF shows in Minneapolis, and I had the opportunity to visit with him, a true class act.

My Last College Game

The week after losing to Texas A&I, I went to the last game of my college career against West Texas State in Amarillo. Although I had spent the week walking on crutches, I couldn't stand the fact that the guys I came in with would be playing without me in their last game. I really loved those guys. So I threw away my crutches and played one more game with the boys. It was a great afternoon. The game meant absolutely nothing in the standings and probably nothing to many people playing. It probably meant nothing to most of the people who came to the game. But it meant something to me. This was my way of saying thanks and good-bye to my friends and coaches who played such a big part in my life and meant so much to me.

Plus, there was a freshman lineman for West Texas that I felt needed a beating before I was out of college.

By the third quarter, my leg was worthless, and I took myself out of the game. By this time, we had the game already won, and I had taught the young freshman a lesson.

I wish I had a fairy-tale ending for this story instead of what actually happened. But that is how life is. When you care very deeply about something, your feelings are at risk. I cared very deeply about Abilene Christian football and about my own success. I was very let down. However, I don't regret one minute, even though we lost that important game. Life to me is about passion, and that is what I had for the game.

It has been said that in grand attempts, even failure is glorious. I think it stinks.

It would have been easier not to care so much, but then success wouldn't mean as much either. Of course, those that don't care don't know much about success. Those people just exist, and are afraid to do much of anything for fear of failure.

Walking On as a Returning All-American

Let's go back one year, to my junior year, to the twenty-second birthday party for my college roommate John Buesing. Being thirsty young men, we had plenty of adult beverages there. We certainly drank our share. This was against Abilene Christian's rules, even though John and I were both of legal drinking age, and it was a private party.

Of course, you can guess the athletic director and dean just loved this. They finally had me. They took away my scholarship and made me pay for my last year of school. I believe I am probably the first returning All-American to have to pay for his senior year. However, ACU wasn't through. While I had spent a year waiting for John Randle, the ACU administration had spent four years hiding in bushes and spying through binoculars, literally, trying to catch me. They sent my roommate and me to counseling. ACU finally had its trophy—me.

In one of the counseling sessions, the counselor was discussing athletics and Jack Youngblood playing with a broken leg for the Los Angeles Rams in the Super Bowl. He stated how bad this was, to risk your health just to accomplish something. Believe me, this counselor will never have to worry about risking his health for anything significant, because cowards like him never have the opportunity. How would you like to have this counselor in a foxhole with you in war, or even have to depend on him at work? He might have the sniffles and decide not to come to work that day.

The average person doesn't care enough about success to be willing to risk everything to achieve it; that's why he is average.

One of my childhood dreams: visiting Loch Ness. It was catch-and-release, or else Nessie would be on my wall.

Don't be average. Be the person who is willing to risk everything. It is a great feeling.

Plan for your future in such a way that you will be able to have the life you want, and if it comes down to it, be willing to put it all on the line. Success doesn't come easy. The more you dream, the more you have to work. Why be average?

It is important to dream, but even more important to plan. Whether you want to be successful in finances or your career, if you don't have a plan, I can promise you won't be successful.

Three Goals

I had my dream, and I had my plan, from a very young age. When I was a freshman in high school at Sweetwater, Texas, I decide that I had three goals in life. One was to be an All-State performer at Sweetwater High. The second was to be an All-American at Abilene Christian. The third was to get the opportunity to play professional football. These may seem an odd lot of goals, but when you realize where I came from, you will understand.

Sweetwater had a tremendous football program, with all the support a local community could muster. In a town of 12,000, we would have up to 8,000 people in attendance at home play-off games. At away games, the town would virtually shut down so that everyone could go. Local football players that did well were talked about in reverent tones for years. High school football was the only show in town, and I wanted to be a part of it. Therefore, goal number one.

The second goal resulted because of the association my family had with Abilene Christian. I can remember going to homecoming football games year after year and wanting to be one of the guys playing. To me, playing for ACU would be the greatest thing that could happen to me. The All-Americans had their pictures hung around the basketball coliseum, and I can remember as a child looking at these pictures with awe. I really wanted to be one of these guys.

The third goal was more understandable. However, very few people from Sweetwater ever made it in the pros. Sammy Baugh was certainly the exception.

The major problem I had when I accomplished goal number three was that I was not very good at football. I don't say this to be modest. It was unfortunately true. When I was a high school freshman, only twelve guys were on the B team, and I was only one of two that didn't get to start both ways on the second team. I had grown very fast, and I was very skinny. That, however, was not the problem. I was also very slow. My speed actually wouldn't pick up until college.

A coach noticed my desire one day. The coach, Charles Copeland, told me that I could fulfill my dreams. I have no idea what he saw, but I am glad he saw it. I worked extremely hard at getting into shape. I hauled hay all summer in the one-hundred-degree heat. I would stick ankle weights down my boots to strengthen my legs. I would run beside the trailer back to the barn. I ran all the time. I would try to load up to three rows of hay on the trailer while the other guys loaded one. I loved the hard work. I'm telling you, the journey is as fun as the destination.

I went to the gym every day, even after working ten to twelve hours. The summer of my junior year I didn't work at all so I could concentrate on training for the football season.

You could say I had a lot at stake. I spent years working on this first of three goals. When you put that much effort into something, the reward is magnified because you know you earned it. I made All-State my senior year at Sweetwater. I even made the All-Texas Super Team, which was a combination of all five high school divisions. The pride I have in that accomplishment is as great as the pride I had in growing up in West Texas, which was a super place for a kid to grow up.

Hanging with the All-Americans

My picture now hangs with all of the other All-Americans at Abilene Christian. I had much more adversity with this second goal, because I never knew I would have to deal with all of the knee surgeries and broken bones. I believe the adversity made me better.

I accomplished my final goal of playing pro football by spending three years between the Los Angeles Raiders and the San Antonio Riders of the World League.

The main thing I had in life, even at an early age, was a clearly defined idea of what I wanted to do. I also had a very clearly defined plan to achieve it.

I have had several great successes in my life. I have also had a few failures. Whether in success or failure, I gave the effort everything I had. When you give it your all, you can live with either outcome. Don't get me wrong, losing still stinks—but you can live with the fact that you failed when you have tried everything possible to succeed. Many people are so afraid of getting hurt that they will never lay anything important on the line. They realize that if you don't have anything at stake, then not accomplishing what you want doesn't bother you as much. In fact, it won't bother you at all.

That is the life of a coward. That is the life of someone who wants to be happy in his current state. He realizes he could fail if he tries something different. The problem is this person isn't truly happy in what he is doing now either. What is worse, he knows he hasn't tried to do anything better.

Make a Difference

If you were to die right now, would your life be complete? Would you feel you had a worthwhile existence? If you are not completely happy with where you are now, then what are you doing about it? Think down the road five to ten years. Will you have started doing the things you wanted to do? You control your future.

The world has enough leeches. Do something to make a difference. If you don't, you are just stealing oxygen from the rest of us.

Big Van Vader

Leave this world better than you found it. One of the kindest things that happened to me was a gift from Leon White (Big Van Vader). In his prime, Leon was one of the sport's great big men, establishing a great career. I had the privilege of wrestling him in his last Pay-Per-View match. Leon was retiring from WWE and would wrestle the rest of his career in Japan, where he was highly revered.

Leon came to me before the match and told me that he was going to give me everything he had that night. He told me he was going to try to turn back the clock and give me the old Vader one last time. What he was saying was that since this was his last match and I was scheduled to win, he wanted it to mean something. He was going to resurrect the monster that was Vader one last time.

Leon did this because of his pride in what he did, and the fact that he liked me. This was his way of passing the torch. I have respected him for this ever since. That was a great thing he did for me. Leon even called in the finish of the match that night that he would hit me with the signature move that he had beaten everyone with, and I would kick out before losing. I would then beat him with *my* finish, which—out of respect for him—I used twice.

Leon left me with a great feeling toward him for what he did. One day it will become my turn to pass the torch. I will gladly do it. The only thing you leave in life are memories. Leave good ones.

USO Tour, Christmas 2002: me, Jeff Jarrett (Soir), Karri Turner, Sergeant Major of the Army Jack Tilley, and Darryl Worley (without his groundhog).

I hope that the next thirty-six years of my life will be as gratifying as the first thirty-six. I have gotten to visit fifty countries and all fifty states. I have had the honor of visiting our great military in the war zones of Afghanistan, Kuwait, and Uzbekistan.

I have had the privilege of swimming in the Indian Ocean with great white sharks, visited Zulu land with my friend Barry Windham, dined with the Yakuza (who were very gracious) in Japan, been served drinks in Buckingham Palace, eaten reindeer in Finland and kangaroo in Australia, rode camels in Oman, watched my wife ride one in Egypt, swum in the Danube, made a hole in one in Athens with my good friends watching, and had countless other experiences.

I have had the good fortune to escape unhurt from a train wreck in Sweden, a crash landing in Birmingham, numerous riots following wrestling shows, and many bar fights.

I don't say this to brag about what I've done; I say it so that you will realize you can do so much more if you are willing to just do it. So many things I thought I didn't have the money or time to do, and I did anyway. These are some of my greatest memories. Live every breath you take; anybody can watch life go by. Be the one people watch.

Use your money to make your life and the lives of those around you better. When you die, you leave everything behind—your money for someone else to spend and your memories for others to cherish. Make your stay here on Earth worthwhile.

I hope you reach all of your goals, and all of the happiness of life reaches you. God bless.

Summary

- **Live, don't just exist.**

ACKNOWLEDGMENTS

Many people have greatly helped me get to where I am and become who I have become. To these people I am eternally gratefully.

I would like to thank a few of my first coaches in high school at Sweetwater and college at Abilene: Charles Copeland and Harvey Oaxaca from Sweetwater, and of course, my favorite coach of all time, Bob Shipley from Abilene. They taught me to never accept being average.

I would like to thank a few of my college buddies who have remained my lifelong friends and always encouraged me in whatever I was doing: John Buesing, Mark McIntyre, Richard Van Druten and Steve Royal.

I have to thank several people who got me started in this terrific business of wrestling: Brad Rheingans, James Beard, and Skandor Akbar.

A world of thanks goes to those guys who have been my tag team partners, best friends and mentors: Barry Windham, Dick Murdoch, Bobby Duncum Jr., Black Bart, and Ron Simmons.

I have worked for two of the greatest bosses in the world, Otto Wanz and Peter William. But none compare to Vince McMahon and the McMahon family. Vince once told me when I was in trouble that he wouldn't lecture me like a son, but that he didn't mind if I would've been. Those kind words have stuck with me all these years and will until I am gone. He's a great man who has taken great care of me and my family.

Several people have helped me a great deal also; Tony St. Clair, Dave Finley, and Mick McMichael in Europe were some of my best friends and greatest teachers.

Bruce Prichard hired me years ago and has been a great friend ever since. Jim Ross has been one of my bosses now for a long time; everyone should have the enjoyment of working for someone of his caliber. Jack Lanza took me under his wing years ago, and if there is anyone I would emulate in this business it would be him. He is what is good about this business. I simply don't know a better person.

A few more guys here in WWE have really helped me as well: Jerry Briscoe has been a friend of mine since day one, and a great help. I am proud to call the Oklahoman (just like I am J.R.) my friend. Undertaker has not only been the cornerstone of this company for the whole time I have been here, but he has been one of my most trusted friends and someone for whom my respect knows no bounds. He *is* the WWE. Also, Steve Austin, who named my finishing move, and has always been there to drink an adult libation and give me advice. Steve's popularity has made the company and me a lot of money. Through it all, he has remained the same friend to me he always has been.

I also would like to thank my sister, Sylvia Sims, for helping me in some of the first edits of my book. A special thanks to Margaret Clark, the executive editor from Pocket Books, for being so kind to a first-time author, and also for being so good.

NET WORTH FINANCIAL WORKSHEET

ASSETS: The Good Part

SAVINGS:	$
INVESTMENTS:	$
HOUSE VALUE:	$
VEHICLES:	$
FURNISHINGS:	$
OTHER:	$
TOTAL:	$

LIABILITIES: The Bad Part

MORTGAGE:	$
CAR LOANS:	$
OTHER LOANS:	$
CREDIT CARDS:	$
TOTAL:	$

TOTAL ASSETS:	$
-TOTAL LIABILITIES:	$
TOTAL NET WORTH:	$

MONTHLY EXPENDITURE WORKSHEET

MORTGAGE OR RENT: $ _____

CABLE OR SATELLITE: $ _____

CAR LOANS: $ _____

INSURANCE
   (car, health, home, other): $ _____

UTILITIES
   (gas, electric, water): $ _____

PHONE: $ _____

OTHER LOANS: $ _____

CREDIT CARD PAYMENTS: $ _____

OTHER PAYMENTS
   (layaways, boat,
   household appliances, etc.): $ _____

TOTAL: $ _____